Implementing the Whole Curriculum for Pupils with Learning Difficulties

Edited by
Richard Rose, Ann Fergusson,
Caroline Coles, Richard Byers and David Banes

David Fulton Publishers

London

NOV94

David Fulton Publishers Ltd
2 Barbon Close, London WC1N 3JX

First published in Great Britain by
David Fulton Publishers 1994

British Library Cataloguing in Publication Data

A catalogue record for this book is available from the British Library

ISBN 1-85346-272-1

Designed by Almac Ltd, London
Typeset by ROM-Data Corporation Limited, Falmouth, Cornwall
Printed in Great Britain by the Cromwell Press, Melksham

Contents

Contributors

Richard Rose, Ann Fergusson, Caroline Coles, Richard Byers and David Banes, the editors of this book, were all members of the National Curriculum Development Team (pupils with severe learning difficulties), together with Jan Tyne, Hazel Lawson, Sandra Galloway, Will Fletcher and Lorraine Cooper. The team was based at Cambridge Institute of Education under the direction of Judy Sebba from 1989 to 1991 and engaged in school-based development work throughout the Eastern region and beyond. Much of this work was reflected in *Curriculum Guidance 9: The National Curriculum and Pupils with Severe Learning Difficulties* and the associated INSET resource pack which were prepared by the team and published by National Curriculum Council in 1992.

The influence of the team's experience in schools was also felt in Hazel Lawson's *Practical Record Keeping for Special Schools* and in Judy Sebba, Richard Byers and Richard Rose's *Redefining the Whole Curriculum for Pupils with Learning Difficulties*. The latter volume explored the theoretical background for much of the practical work described in the following chapters.

David Banes is senior teacher at Meldreth Manor, an independent residential school in Hertfordshire. Meldreth Manor, which caters for pupils with physical disabilities and severe and profound and multiple learning difficulties, is run by the Spastics Society.

Richard Byers teaches at Riverwalk, a school for pupils with severe learning difficulties in Bury St. Edmunds, Suffolk.

Sue Chesworth heads the further education department at Belstead School in Ipswich, Suffolk. Belstead caters for pupils with severe learning difficulties.

Caroline Coles is headteacher at Meldreth Manor School.

Ann Fergusson is deputy headteacher at Windmill School in Cambridge. Windmill caters for pupils with severe learning difficulties.

Will Fletcher is head of upper school at Watling View, a school for pupils with severe learning difficulties in St. Albans, Hertfordshire.

Sandra Galloway is head of lower school at Watling View.

Judith Gordon teaches in the further education unit of Watling View School.

Joanne Hardwick teaches in the seniors department of Greenside, a school for pupils with severe learning difficulties in Stevenage, Hertfordshire.

Joy Hardwick heads the secondary department at Wren Spinney School for pupils with severe learning difficulties in Kettering, Northamptonshire.

Hazel Lawson heads the seniors department at Greenside School.

Richard Rose is headteacher of Wren Spinney School.

Peter Rushton is deputy headteacher of Wren Spinney School.

Judy Sebba is tutor in special educational needs at the University of Cambridge Institute of Education.

Jan Tyne is an independent teacher and adviser specialising in advocacy issues for people with learning difficulties.

Acknowledgements

The authors wish to acknowledge the ideas, support and co-operation of all the pupils and staff in the many schools who have influenced our work. The editors would further like to thank the Director and staff of the University of Cambridge Institute of Education for providing continued support for our work since our time as members of the National Curriculum Development Team and the staff at Meldreth Manor School, who have provided hospitality for meetings.

The views expressed in this book are those of the individual authors and should not be seen as representative of any organisation within which they are currently employed.

Foreword
Judy Sebba

I have always imagined that writing forewords, like chairing conferences, was what you are invited to do when you are 'past your peak'. Ignoring this possibility, I shall try to set the context for what follows in the light of what has been. In *Redefining the Whole Curriculum for Pupils with Learning Difficulties* (Sebba, Byers and Rose, 1993) we provided more questions than answers. We aimed to be provocative and ideological in order to challenge current classroom practice and create a little discomfort in those who have not had the time or inclination to stop and question their well-established methods. We hoped to get away with this by promising a second volume with practical examples of what we had preached.

We did not get off so lightly. One review (MacConville and Bowers, 1993) described it as 'an unfortunate stance ... interesting and useful texts are normally able to combine good theory and practice'. Another reviewer (Thomas, 1993) was more concerned with the style than the content and decided to talk to his daughter's guinea pig on the grounds that it would make more sense. He may find that chapter 9 in this volume provides useful guidelines on animal habitation. Other reviewers were more positive about our success in challenging assumptions that underlie current practice.

We have kept our promise. This volume is the hard work of practising teachers, which is the real reason why, as an ivory tower university lecturer, I was unable to contribute. The main themes from the previous volume are illustrated by descriptions of ongoing work in schools. Since we cannot assume familiarity with the previous volume, I have identified these themes here.

Theme 1 : All pupils have a legal entitlement to a broad and balanced curriculum but this does not ensure access in practice

While the Education Reform Act legislated for entitlement, access in practice is much harder to achieve. In 1993, OFSTED reported that although teachers were strongly committed to the provision of full access to the National Curriculum for all pupils, 'almost half the pupils in special schools were still not receiving a satisfactorily broad and balanced curriculum which complied with National Curriculum requirements' (OFSTEDc, 1993, p.3). This volume provides many examples of ways in which access can be enhanced even for those pupils whose multiple disabilities present the greatest challenge. Chapters 7 on communication and 8 on information technology cover two major areas through which access can be developed.

Theme 2 : The whole curriculum is more than just the National Curriculum and the relationship between the parts of the whole curriculum will need to be flexible enough to cope with changing individual needs

We suggested that the relationship between the National Curriculum, the traditional developmental curriculum and additional curricular aspects such as therapies, will vary from pupil to pupil and for the same pupil over time. In this volume, chapter 4 on auditing provides practical approaches to monitoring what curriculum is being delivered, chapter 5 describes a modular curriculum approach which enables teachers to collaborate in achieving breadth and balance and chapter 10 illustrates one school's approach to ensuring relevant information on each of these three aspects of the whole curriculum is recorded. Chapter 2 describes an example of an appropriate curriculum for a senior department in which breadth and balance are maintained and continuity provided from National Curriculum work covered in the school.

Theme 3 : Teaching approaches need to balance group work and individual needs and create greater opportunity for pupil directed learning

The previous volume was interpreted by some teachers as an attack on individualised, objectives-based curricula. It attempted to argue that individual priorities could be addressed within group work and in the context of activities which might relate to the National Curriculum. An emphasis on problem solving was seen as requiring the teacher to take risks through more pupil-directed learning. The story of the 'crazy teacher' in chapter 9 of this volume provides a humorous but true example of how this might be put into practice.

Theme 4 : Effective management of the whole curriculum must involve parents, professionals and the pupils themselves

Every chapter in this volume addresses pupil involvement and provides examples of this in practice. Chapter 6 describes the role of parents and other professionals (in addition to the pupil), in determining the curriculum for each pupil and its effective delivery. The importance of teamwork and the transmission of specialist skills to staff in daily contact with the pupil, emerge clearly from this chapter.

Theme 5 : Personal and social development, as distinct from traditional views of personal and social education, should permeate throughout the curriculum and ethos of the school

This theme in the previous volume was by far the most contentious with readers' views heavily polarised. This volume provides illustrations of what personal and social development for pupils with learning difficulties means in practice and links it to themes of 'education for life'. Chapter 3 describes a programme with older students designed to explore attitudes, feelings and behaviour. Chapter 12 covers advocacy and chapter 11, records of achievement in practice. This chapter brings us full circle back to issues of access, by illustrating ways in which access to the Records of Achievement process might be meaningfully established for pupils with multiple disabilities.

The issues in this book are not specific to the current National Curriculum, or indeed, any National Curriculum. The debate about what and how pupils with learning difficulties should be taught will continue in the context of future changes in the legally defined curriculum. The message in this book is clear - ask the pupils!

Preface

This book, which fulfils the promise made by Sebba, Byers and Rose to provide examples of practice built upon the principles described in *Redefining the Whole Curriculum for Pupils with Learning Difficulties* (1993), has been written by teachers who are attempting to move the current curriculum debate forward through good practice. The chapters within this book can do no more than provide examples from the wealth of good practice which exists in schools, where teachers of pupils with learning difficulties have looked beyond the confines of the National Curriculum to ensure that the needs of groups and individual pupils are met through the development of the whole curriculum.

Since this is a sister volume to *Redefining the Whole Curriculum for Pupils with Learning Difficulties*, we have chosen to follow most of the stylistic conventions which were observed in the first book.

All of the chapters in the following pages have been written from the standpoint of work among pupils and students who experience what are defined as severe learning difficulties. In places the text does reflect the authors' need to be specific with regard to certain pupil groupings, and readers will encounter phrases such as 'pupils with profound and multiple learning difficulties' or 'a pupil who displayed challenging behaviours'. In general, however, we have encouraged the use of the phrase 'pupils with learning difficulties', both because we believe that most of the ideas described in these chapters have a relevance across the broad range of pupils so described and because we await the coining of a better alternative (People First please note!).

We have also continued with the convention of challenging gender stereotypes by referring to pupils as 'she' where a singular pronoun is demanded, and to school staff as 'he'.

We are aware of an anglo-centric bias to the work which is represented here. We acknowledge this as a failing and apologise to people lucky enough not to live in southern England. We would ask readers to note that, in general terms, references to Local Education Authorities can be read to refer to any form of education authority; that a Statement is functionally equivalent to a Record of Special Educational Needs; that Ministers of State are similar creatures to Secretaries of State and that working within the National Curriculum is comparable to working within any nationally agreed curriculum. References to specific items from Orders for specific subjects are comparatively rare in this book, and readers will usually be able to translate the principles behind what is being described into the language of other national curricula.

The chapters here included do not imply that the authors have found an answer, or 'the correct way' to approach the specific areas covered. They are rather intended to provide the reader with practical examples of approaches which have been put into operation in schools with some degree of success.

There is a considerable literature available elsewhere to assist with the teaching of specific subjects (see chapter 1). In collating material for this book, we have preferred to concentrate upon issues which have proved to be of concern to staff working to develop a whole curriculum for pupils with learning difficulties. We believe that it is important to continue to reflect upon those aspects of school life which play a central role in meeting the needs of the whole pupil.

We hope that this book will be read by teachers, classroom assistants, parents, governors, therapists, psychologists and other practitioners involved directly or indirectly with the education of pupils with learning difficulties. Most of all we hope that this book will contribute to the ongoing task of reviewing and refining classroom practice for the benefit of all who share in the learning process.

Richard Rose, Ann Fergusson, Caroline Coles, Richard Byers and David Banes, October, 1993.

Chapter One

Schools Should Decide . . .

Richard Byers and Richard Rose

Redefining the Whole Curriculum for Pupils with Learning Difficulties (Sebba, Byers and Rose, 1993) set out to describe a process of curriculum development which had at least three distinct features:

- the need to retain and revitalise those aspects of traditional curricula still seen as priorities in schools for pupils with learning difficulties;
- the task of developing means of access into and assimilating the demands of the National Curriculum;
- the drive to continue to push forward, alongside colleagues in mainstream schools, into territory concerned with pupils' personal and social development and specifically towards such targets as pupil autonomy, pupil self responsibility, pupil consultation and advocacy.

This introductory chapter reviews some of the work which has ensured meaningful routes into the National Curriculum and given schools a means of integrating new programmes of study with traditional curricular priorities. It also examines some of the recent developments in education and proposes that it is time for school communities to reclaim control over the processes of curriculum development, curriculum management and curriculum implementation. This chapter argues in favour of local ownership of those fundamental principles which underpin and guide the work of school communities in promoting pupils' personal and social development.

Entitlement

In the Acknowledgements at the beginning of *Redefining the Whole Curriculum for Pupils with Learning Difficulties* the authors stated an intention of the book as being 'to motivate teachers and others to question, reflect, and ultimately move their practices forward to the benefit of the pupils with whom they work.' In many respects it was a safe assumption that this would, in fact, happen. What was perhaps less predictable at the time when *Redefining the Whole Curriculum for Pupils with Learning Difficulties* was published, was the intensity of the debate which is currently evident throughout the education system with regards to the curriculum for pupils with learning difficulties.

Staff in schools for pupils with learning difficulties are well used to coping with challenge, difficulty, disappointment and innovation. Indeed, teaching in many schools for pupils with learning difficulties was itself, prior to the Education Reform Act of 1988, a discipline in its infancy. Staff had grown used to assimilating and accommodating new ideas and to operating in a climate of constant improvisation. Indeed, this sense of adaptability lay at the heart of one of the proudest claims of staff in schools for pupils with learning difficulties when receiving pupils who were said to have failed, or at least to have experienced a lack of success, in grappling with the curriculum and work habits insisted upon in mainstream schools. Staff receiving those pupils into schools for pupils with learning difficulties prior to 1988 claimed that they did not operate a curriculum or a set of behavioural codes into which pupils must fit or be rejected. On the contrary, such staff perceived their task as being to devise a curriculum and a code of conduct which would meet the needs of each individual pupil in their charge even if this meant creating a new programme for each and every pupil.

This philosophy of needs driven, individualised education underpinned much of the work of schools for pupils with learning difficulties throughout most of the 1970s and 1980s. The system came to be criticised for its narrowness, but it always maintained a firm claim on relevance. There was a sense that it was good to be different – that schools for pupils with learning difficulties were able to be more true to the spirit of pupil-centred education largely because they were not hidebound by all the restrictions of an imposed curriculum and system of assessment and examination. The rhetoric stated that schools for pupils with learning difficulties operated in a realm of purity and altruism where the benefit of the pupil was the sole guiding influence. It does not need to be said that this claim was naive and patently untrue in many instances, but it did serve as part of the ethical foundation for the work of many members of staff in schools for pupils with learning difficulties and it did engender in those staff a powerful sense of ownership of the curriculum, of methodology and of the spirit and ethos which underpinned the functioning of school communities.

It was this sense of ownership which the Education Reform Act of 1988, with its introduction of the National Curriculum and its associated testing and assessment procedures, most significantly challenged. At a stroke, schools for pupils with learning difficulties were apparently required to conform to the very kind of curriculum and assessment straitjacket which had ensured failure for so many pupils in mainstream schools in the past. Indeed, judging by the initial reactions of many mainstream colleagues, this was to be a more constricting system of restraint than anything which had gone before. The legislation seemed to herald the loss of freedom - not a freedom to do as one pleased, but a freedom to do the best for one's pupils - a freedom which enabled staff in schools for pupils with learning difficulties to provide the most appropriate educational experience for each and every one of their clients. Somewhere close to the heart of this sense of freedom and ownership came the notion that pupils' personal and social development and a grounding in practical living skills were more relevant to pupils' real needs than any subject based curriculum.

It came as no surprise, therefore, when concerns were expressed in the early days following the introduction of the National Curriculum that the needs of pupils with learning difficulties had been largely ignored. Furthermore, the provision of advice for its introduction was in short supply and was the source of some confusion (Wedell, 1988; Norwich, 1989; Ware, 1990). Indeed, the early documentation reflected an Education Reform Act which had been ill conceived, badly constructed, and which, through its speedy introduction, provided general bewilderment for those charged with its implementation. As Brahm Norwich (1989) stated:

> There must be many, who like me, are watching the gradual implementation of the Education Reform Act with increasing bewilderment and wondering how it will work. How will the principle that there should be maximum participation in the National Curriculum by all children, and minimal use of the statutory exceptions, be reconciled with the practical realities of operating a new curricular framework ? (p. 94)

Understandably, the outcry from teachers of pupils with learning difficulties was considerable. The Act's statement of entitlement had to a large extent been overlooked by those charged with a responsibility to structure the National Curriculum. Wider concerns were expressed about the intentions of an Education Act which appeared to be driven by political motivation rather than establishing its roots within sound educational theory. This was a feeling further enhanced by what appeared to be an inability to address with any understanding the issues of assessment and testing when related to pupils with learning difficulties. As Peter Mittler stated in his Foreword to *Entitlement for All in Practice* (Fagg, Aherne, Skelton and Thornber, 1990):

> In their preoccupation with raising standards and in winning public confidence, children with special educational needs could easily be forgotten or marginalised. Where children with severe learning difficulties are concerned there are real fears that exclusion from the National Curriculum could be tantamount to exclusion from the education service. (p. 11)

The majority of teachers have come to regard entitlement as a key issue in addressing the needs of all pupils within the framework of the National Curriculum. The debate goes far beyond finding means of accessing the National Curriculum for all pupils, though this in itself is a matter which continues to warrant our closest attention. Issues which must be confronted centre upon the whole curriculum, and ensuring that the education provided for pupils with learning difficulties continues to recognise individuality and to address needs beyond those identified within the core and other foundation subjects structure. A legitimate argument has been advanced which fears that recent legislation will dilute the curriculum offered to pupils with learning difficulties, detracting from the essential elements developed by staff in schools over a number of years (Staff of Tye Green School, 1991; Ware, 1990). At the extreme end of this argument is the notion than pupils with learning difficulties, and in particular those with severe learning difficulties, should be removed entirely from the National Curriculum. Others (Pease and Chapman, 1992) have suggested that we should begin by disapplying pupils with learning difficulties from the National Curriculum, and then considering a form of opting-in to those aspects which may be considered appropriate for some pupils. To follow this line, we would argue, would be to set a dangerous precedent. The Education Reform Act was, in fact, the first educational legislation which attempted to embrace all pupils, maintaining the right of *every pupil* to a broad, balanced, relevant, and well differentiated curriculum. As argued by Mittler (above) exclusion of any group of pupils from this right would provide an early step on the path to exclusion from the broader education system.

Within the area of special education, the National Curriculum has certainly been a catalyst for controversy and debate. Opinions on the content of the curriculum and the response which teachers of pupils with learning difficulties should make to the National Curriculum have been diverse and have promoted much discussion. What cannot be questioned is the motivation of those teachers who have been at the forefront of this debate to provide a better and more effective education for the pupils in their charge.

Access

One of the, presumably unintended, side effects of the Education Reform Act of 1988 was to engender in staff in schools for pupils with learning difficulties a palpable sense of having been de-skilled, dis-enfranchised and dis-empowered. This in some instances led to alienation, withdrawal, suspicion and hostility - a surprising set of responses to legislation which, as we have established, set out to emphasise access and entitlement, and hence inclusion, for all pupils within the same curriculm. Part of this reaction can be attributed to subject phobia - a phenomenon shared by many mainstream colleagues faced with the prospect of being required to teach science, technology or a modern foreign language, for example, when these subjects existed only as distant and hazy personal memories of one's own school career.

But there was more to it than that. To feel inadequately prepared in the face of teaching unfamiliar or hazily remembered subjects is a form of de-skilling which can be, has been and is being remedied in various ways all over the country. The introduction of the National Curriculum has provided new opportunities for teachers to reflect upon their existing practices, and to re-examine both the content of the curriculum offered in schools, and the way in which it is delivered. Teachers of pupils with learning difficulties, as ever, have been innovative in their approaches to curriculum change. They have not only addressed the challenges of the National Curriculum, but have also responded to the requirements for breadth, balance and relevance by questioning as-sumptions made by recent legislation, and by demonstrating, through classroom practice, the value of providing a wider curriculum focus for all pupils. Understandable apprehensions concerning the relevance of the National Curriculum for pupils with learning difficulties have not been ignored. From a common standpoint of wishing to improve the education provided to pupils with learning difficulties, a purposeful variety of approaches and attitudes has developed.

Early in the debate, teachers who were concerned to ensure that pupils with learning difficulties received their full entitlement to access to the National Curriculum, began to demonstrate ways in which the specific subject documents could be used to good effect. This was achieved despite a lack of guidance, or anything more than passing references to the needs of pupils with learning difficulties in the original National Curriculum documentation. In contrast, the work of the Manchester City Council Education Department Teacher Fellows amply demonstrated ways in which the core subject areas could be implemented when working with pupils with learning difficulties. Within a short time of the introduction of each of the core and other foundation subjects, further examples were published of ways in which teachers sought to provide access to the National Curriculum for pupils with learning difficulties (Aherne, Thornber, Fagg and Skelton, 1990a; 1990b; Fagg, Skelton, Aherne and Thornber, 1990; Howe, 1991; Sebba and Clarke, 1991; 1993; Rose, 1992; Mount and Ackerman, 1991; Banes and Sebba, 1991).

Thanks to the pioneering work of authors such as these and the impact it has had upon professional development, there is a new generation of subject specialist teachers out there in schools for pupils with learning difficulties - science teachers who declare themselves, confidently and cheerfully, as 'non-scientists' and folk teaching technology who will admit blithely that they cannot put up a shelf. Staff are making the National Curriculum their own. They are coming to ideas with minds fresh and free from preconceptions and facing up to challenges enthusiastically. They are sharing their enthusiasm by creating exciting, effective and liberating schemes of work for their pupils. They have achieved this level of confidence and expertise surprisingly swiftly, partly because there has been effective support through publications and in the form of professional development but mainly by dint of their own hard work and resilience at the chalk face.

This is not to imply that the National Curriculum as it stands is in any way perfect, or currently achieves its stated objective of inclusion for all pupils. Clearly the first editions of the National Curriculum were not written with pupils with learning difficulties in mind. This is a fact already recognised at the highest level. While a common complaint heard in staffrooms has been aimed at the number of changes and the different versions of documents which have been presented to schools, it is generally accepted that later versions have taken note of teacher comments, not least with regard to the needs of pupils with learning difficulties. Responsibility for continuing improvement must rest with all who are concerned to improve the education of those pupils. As Sebba and Fergusson (1991) have stated:

If the National Curriculum is not appropriate for these pupils as it stands, then it may be necessary to suggest ways in which it could be revised to meet the needs of all pupils rather than taking pupils out of the system. This is surely implied by an entitlement curriculum and will be a necessary step in ensuring marginalisation is reduced. (p. 212)

To its credit, the National Curriculum Council did begin to address the issues raised by teachers of pupils with learning difficulties. As National Curriculum documents have been reissued they have contained guidance designed to assist in teaching pupils with special needs. The work of the National Curriculum Development Team, based at the University of Cambridge Institute of Education informed and influenced documentation which was published by the National Curriculum Council (NCC, 1992a, 1992b, 1992c) with a specific focus upon pupils with learning difficulties. Opportunities have been given for teachers both individually and collectively to express their views and provide ideas on how the National Curriculum can be applied when working with all pupils with special needs. Professional Officers from the National Curriculum Council and from the Schools Examination and Assessment Council (SEAC) have made efforts to visit schools and groups of teachers and have listened to their views. It is now the responsibility of all teachers to ensure that the pressure brought to bear upon the National Curriculum Council and the Schools Examination and Assessment Council to ensure inclusion of all pupils is maintained upon the Schools Curriculum and Assessment Authority (SCAA). Sir Ron Dearing, Chairman of SCAA, has signalled his intention to take note of such pressure. In his interim report on *The National Curriculum and its Assessment,* Sir Ron (1993b) acknowledges that:

> . . . teachers have stressed that it is important for pupils with special educational needs to benefit from the breadth of the National Curriculum but they believe that it contains too much content. In the work on slimming down the curriculum, therefore, it will be crucial to take account of the views of such teachers to ensure that their pupils can enjoy full access to the National Curriculum. (p. 33)

Breadth

It has been interesting to note the ways in which the more prescriptive aspects of the legislation and guidance associated with the National Curriculum have been eroded over the years since 1988. There were times when it seemed that the relative proportions of the school week allocated to different subjects on the timetable would be dictated to schools. There have been times when staff in schools have braced themselves for the imposition of an approved selection of styles of teaching in which many tried, tested and favoured methods would be outlawed. There have been times when subject specialists have feared that their discipline would be reduced to a narrow extract of facts, figures or fragments for pupils to memorise in the name of a return to the educational standards of some mythical time in the past. It has consistently seemed that the curriculum would become swamped by a system of assessment procedures of oceanic proportions. During these times, staff in schools for pupils with learning difficulties have striven assiduously to look for, and sometimes have found, the silver lining in the most threatening of clouds. In many senses, these people have been in the vanguard of a movement to maintain, even perhaps to introduce, balance and variety within the whole curriculum. This has been expressed in the eagerness with which they have greeted the wide range of materials designed to render the subjects of the National Curriculum accessible, both to pupils with learning difficulties and to their teachers, and through a firm determination to increase rather than reduce the spectrum of teaching approaches available for staff to use.

Part of the impetus behind this movement has been the desire to maintain ownership of the whole curriculum in order to ensure its continuing relevance to pupils with learning difficulties. Somewhat unexpectedly, 1993 saw official recognition of the wisdom and desirability of encouraging school communities to retain this level of ownership and this degree of control over decisions about the management and delivery of the curriculum. The first indications that the argument was officially over came when the Office for Standards in Education (OFSTED) published its response to Alexander, Rose and Woodhead's report on *Curriculum Organisation and Classroom Practice in Primary Schools* (1992). OFSTED (1993a) noted that 'the vast majority of primary schools remain committed to grouping aspects of different subjects together to be taught as "topics" ' and that 'about two-thirds of schools had a satisfactory balance between topics and separate subjects.' This acknowledgement of the reality that schools seek to provide a balanced range of approaches to teaching was endorsed in *The National Curriculum at Key Stages 1 and 2* (NCC, 1993a), which suggested that schools should make 'decisions about which elements within the National Curriculum are best taught through subjects and which through well-focused topics.'

The National Curriculum Council then published *Planning the National Curriculum at Key Stage 2* (NCC, 1993b). This document emerged quietly onto the educational stage as one of the last items of 'official' National Curriculum Council guidance immediately prior to the act of fusion which resulted in the creation of the School Curriculum and Assessment Authority. *Planning the National Curriculum at Key Stage 2* contained within its pages a number of distinctly interesting proposals. It suggested that the staff in schools should themselves decide how much of the available timetable should be devoted to the 'basic curriculum', in other words, the core and other foundation subjects of the National Curriculum plus religious education, and how much set aside for 'other aspects of the curriculum'. True, the examples given in the document do not represent any radical departure from a situation in which the timetable is dominated by the National Curriculum, but they do suggest that varying proportions of each week, as well as whole chunks of time measured in days or even weeks of each school year, should be devoted to special events, extra-curricular activities and other aspects of the whole curriculum.

Further, the document proposes that it is for staff in schools to decide upon the emphasis they give to each subject of the National Curriculum in the light of the perceived needs of groups of pupils. Again, the examples used in the book to illustrate this process are unsurprisingly conformist, but they do show real decisions being made about balance within the whole curriculum, decisions which, for instance, result in some subjects not appearing on the timetable at all in weeks when priority is given to other, more important, pupil needs. Of course, these sorts of decisions are to be made in the light of the requirement that all legally defined aspects of each subject should be taught at some time, but the fact that the National Curriculum Council endorses the devolution of this measure of control to school level is significant and possibly particularly encouraging for staff in schools for pupils with learning difficulties.

Planning the National Curriculum at Key Stage 2 takes this devolution of control further still. It suggests that decisions about how to teach the subjects of the National Curriculum should also be made at school level. It suggests that some aspects of some subjects will probably need to be taught continuously through a pupil's school career while other material may be presented as finite 'blocked units of work' or modules. It also proposes that staff should make their own decisions about how 'curriculum coherence can be strengthened by linking together, where appropriate, units from different subjects'. The authors suggest that teachers 'need to decide when to use separate subject teaching as opposed to a topic approach' and suggest that:

> well-planned topic work which is focused on a limited range of specific aspects of the Orders and religious education can be an effective way of organising the curriculum. (p. 24)

The document closes with the suggestion that the plans arrived at using the structures proposed in the book should be maintained under 'whole staff review' each year.

Balance

In his Foreword to *Planning the National Curriculum at Key Stage 2* Sir Ron Dearing (1993a) acknowledges that 'the two most valuable resources schools possess' are 'teaching time and the expertise of the teaching staff.' In giving his seal of approval to this document, which enshrines principles of school-level planning, implementation and ownership of the curriculum, Sir Ron prefigures many of the conclusions which he himself reached in the course of his review of curriculum and testing arrangements during 1993.

Sir Ron Dearing's interim report, *The National Curriculum and its Assessment* (Dearing, 1993b), offers 'recognition that the professional judgement of teachers must be trusted' and argues for a structure which will 'allow teachers to exercise their professional judgement.' Sir Ron peppers his report with examples of the ways in which this redistribution of control over the curriculum, its management, its implementation and associated assessment and reporting regimes, should be returned in large measure to school staff. He recommends 'giving equal status to teacher assessment and to national tests in reporting to parents and others', itself a highly significant step away from the entrenched positions held by ministers through the first years of the nineties. Sir Ron is also clear in his views on the debate about teaching approaches. He states, categorically, that schools should 'of course, continue to make their own decisions on whether the curriculum is best organised in terms of individual subjects or well-focused and structured topics or some mixture of the two' just as if there had never been any centrally driven attempt to prescribe ways of delivering the curriculum which were ideologically acceptable to adherents of a narrow political point of view.

But Sir Ron goes further. He embraces a vision of a flexible curriculum, similar to that presented in *Planning the National Curriculum at Key Stage 2,* and extends it. Not only does he note that students entering Key Stage 4 'want to determine their own futures' and 'expect their education to reflect their individual interests and talents', he also makes a case for a 'less prescriptive' and 'reduced' National Curriculum. Sir Ron proposes that:

> elements of the Orders should be specified as optional so that schools can decide, in the light of local circumstance, the professional expertise of

teachers and the needs of their pupils, the extent to which they draw upon this additional material. (page 29)

This flexibility should be available to schools within 'a clear policy framework' which establishes 'an appropriate margin of time' to be devoted to learning beyond the statutory basic curriculum. Simply to find phrases such as 'professional judgement' being used in official publications might indicate that events have moved closer towards a return to control over the balance of aspects within the whole curriculum operating at a local level. As Sir Ron Dearing reminds us, this control properly rests in the hands of school staff, parents, governors and, significantly, the pupils themselves.

Relevance

This view of the curriculum echoes that presented in chapter 2 of *Redefining the Whole Curriculum for Pupils with Learning Difficulties*, where readers were encouraged to adopt a 'realistic and flexible approach to implementing the National Curriculum', and raises one of the major issues explored in many of the chapters in this volume. One of the purposes of this book is to empower school staff with a sense that it is possible and desirable to re-establish control over the curriculum. Another of its purposes is to suggest that such control should be shared, certainly with parents and governors, but also with pupils.

Those who regard this as an admirable but unattainable ideal, should bear in mind the extent to which the philosophy and practice of power-sharing and consultation is being cast in statute. The *Handbook for the Inspection of Schools* (OFSTED, 1993b) continually emphasises that pupils must be active participants in planning, implementing and evaluating their own learning. Indeed the document establishes the principle that pupils should be consulted, along with parents and governors, as part of the process of inspecting schools against OFSTED criteria. At every turn, including within those sections dealing with judgements to be made about 'management and administration', 'standards of achievement', 'quality of teaching', 'assessment, recording and reporting' and 'quality and range of the curriculum', inspectors are reminded that 'evidence should include . . . discussion with . . . pupils.' This general requirement to seek pupils' views is expressed in more detail in many sections of both the *Framework for the Inspection of Schools* and the *Guidance on the Inspection Schedule.* In a section on 'pupils' personal development and behaviour' in the *Guidance,* it is stated that:

discussions with pupils should enable inspectors to judge . . . whether the quality of relationships is such that pupils feel free to express and explore their views openly and honestly. (page 16)

Two of the evaluation criteria for 'quality of teaching' are that 'teachers have clear objectives for their lessons' and that 'pupils are aware of these objectives' (page 27). The intention is even expressed in the *Framework*, in a section on 'behaviour and discipline', that pupils' views should be represented in inspectors' final reports:

The report should include... a clear indication of... the way in which pupils react to school rules and conventions... together with evaluation of... pupils' and parents' responses to the application of any system of rewards and sanctions. (page 24).

In case there are any doubts as to whether these kinds of statements apply generally, a section dealing specifically with pupils with special educational needs insists that 'the entire *Framework* applies to the inspection of special schools.' Further, the section makes it clear that the evidence which will assist inspectors in evaluating:

the quality of learning and standards achieved by pupils with special educational needs... should include... discussion with staff, pupils and parents (page 33),

while the Guidance insists that:

procedures and practice for assessment, recording and reporting should... involve the appropriate teachers, support professionals, parents and the pupils themselves. (page 62)

Thus the inspection criteria echo the views of commentators such as Tilstone (1991), in seeking to encourage professionals to listen and respond to the voice of the pupil, and the Special Education Consortium (Peter, 1993) in endorsing the notion of pupil consultation in their attempts to bring the Code of Practice relating to the 1993 Education Act more closely into line with the requirements of the 1989 Children Act.

Conclusion

It is heartening to see the extent to which these concerns are made explicit in OFSTED's inspection criteria. The very fact that a major section in the *Framework for the Inspection of Schools* deals with 'pupils' spiritual, moral, social and cultural development' as revealed in 'the quality of relationships between pupils and adults' and 'the opportunities for, and quality of, pupils' contributions to the school' indicates that pupils' personal and social development will need to remain high on the agenda for all schools. It also offers support, from a somewhat unexpected direction, for the position adopted by the editors of this book.

The curriculum is an ever changing entity. It must reflect the current climate in schools and the wider community. In order that it may fulfil its main purpose, that of providing a sound education as a right of all pupils, it is essential that staff within those schools learn from one another and share their experiences and ideas. It is to be hoped that the introduction of local management of special schools will not drive school communities into competition - competition over the 'best' documentation, perhaps, or even over the placement of those potential pupils who are seen as offering the most promising financial returns. Schools must insist that they will continue to act in the best interests of their pupils, even where this does not make good 'business' sense. There should be no relaxation in the drive towards integration; no compromise over educationally appropriate pupil placements; no reduction in the willingness of schools to share and collaborate. We hope that the sharing of some of the ideas and approaches described within this volume may be of help to staff striving to tackle the complexities of the whole curriculum within their own schools.

Inevitably, this book will raise as many questions as it answers. It remains to be seen, for instance, exactly how OFSTED inspectors will make judgements about the quality of teacher-pupil relationships or about the outcomes of learning where pupils experience profound and multiple learning difficulties. As was recently revealed in correspondence to *PMLD Link* (Summer 1993), inspectors of schools appear to be sadly ill-prepared to interpret the criteria for the identification of effective learning in some groups of pupils. It will also be intriguing to observe inspectors going about the business of consulting with those pupils in order to gain some insight into their impressions of the education they receive. As with the introduction of the National Curriculum, it is to be hoped that the task will be to find means of access on behalf of those pupils rather than to deny their entitlement to participate in this new level of educational endeavour. And as with the long process of rendering entitlement to the National Curriculum meaningful by evolving access routes through a broad, balanced, relevant whole curriculum, it is fervently to be hoped that these developments will be school-led, school-driven and school-owned. In the end, school communities, including staff, governors, parents and pupils, *should* decide.

15

Chapter Two

Developing a Curriculum for the Seniors Department

Hazel Lawson and Joanne Hardwick

We would like to acknowledge the work of the staff at Greenside School, Hertfordshire.

The authors both work as teachers in a school for pupils with severe learning difficulties. The work described here was developed by staff working with students in the seniors department. This process has included input from speech therapists and the staff equal opportunities representative. More recently the students have been involved in developing an additional curriculum guide.

Introduction

We intend this chapter to be a practical and informative account of the development of a curriculum/curriculum document for use in the seniors department of a school for pupils with severe learning difficulties. The chapter forms part of the review and development process of our working curriculum document and is, therefore, a form of evaluation. We also intend it to be a source of information for others involved in curriculum development.

We acknowledge the broad definition of the curriculum embraced by Sebba, Byers and Rose (1993); the work we describe here will be concerned with that part of the curriculum defined as the *planned* learning experiences in school (Pring, 1990).

The curriculum document is intended as a representation of this practice, providing a framework and source of guidance and reference for teaching and learning.

Reasons for developing the seniors curriculum

The curriculum continues to evolve. This chapter focuses on a time span of three years, from its conception to the present day. A number of factors determined the need to develop the curriculum and accompanying curriculum document.

- The school was operating on two sites and, prior to the amalgamation, neither site had recent, relevant documentation. The development of a document was intended to be a positive team building exercise to encourage a common sense of purpose and structure in the new seniors department. The process of development was a useful starting point for us, as a team, to pool our ideas and beliefs.
- The document was developed as part of our increasing accountability as a means of describing and justifying what we do in a variety of learning situations.
- By developing the seniors curriculum we hoped we would enhance our knowledge and awareness and be able to include and build upon the National Curriculum. We previously had National Curriculum working groups for the core subjects and we hoped to incorporate that work into our documentation.
- We wanted to consider the curriculum being offered to the seniors in general and to each pupil in particular. This necessitated looking at issues of breadth, balance and differentiation.
- We felt the document would be a source of information for staff, pupils, parents, governors and other professionals.

The process of development

Meetings were held on a regular basis, both after school and on in-service training days, involving staff from the two school sites. All staff working with students of the senior age range were invited. Informal minutes were taken to ensure all staff were kept informed and to keep a record of discussion points and decisions made.

For the first year, we concentrated on the curriculum for sixteen to nineteen year old students (years 12 to 14) with severe learning difficulties. However, as the structure of the new school took shape, several factors needed to be considered. These included class organisation according to chronological age, student numbers and the physical arrangement of buildings and classroom facilities. The new seniors department would cover age range fourteen to nineteen (years 10 to 14). This entailed greater consideration of National Curriculum areas at Key Stage 4.

Entitlement

We began by discussing the entitlements of all students, based on a list of entitlements compiled by the local Technical and Vocational Education Initiative (TVEI) consortium. This had the advantage of being neutral to staff from each site. It started with ideas rather than practicalities so we were able to share our feelings about principles underlying our teaching and it gave us an immediate link with mainstream school developments. The following list of entitlements for all students was agreed:

- equality of opportunity
- self advocacy
- record of achievement
- numeracy
- communication
- science/technology
- information technology
- economic/industrial/enviromental awareness
- social/political/cultural awareness
- aesthetic awareness
- work experience/insight to work
- industrial links and enterprise
- guidance and counselling (including careers)
- values and attitudes
- creative skills
- problem solving
- leisure/recreational activities
- physical development
- integration.

Curriculum areas

We felt it important to have a cross-curricular approach within which a student's individual curriculum 'diet' would be developed. However we still found it necessary to identify different curriculum areas as a basis for planning, recording and reporting and for organising curriculum documentation. These were based upon the areas we had previously used and on those defined by Dee (1988).

It took much discussion to agree upon curriculum areas; the names for areas were frequently disputed and altered to reflect current thinking.

The current agreed curriculum areas are:

- personal, health and social education
- communication (including National Curriculum English)
- mathematics (including National Curriculum)
- science (including National Curriculum)
- technology (including National Curriculum)
- humanities (including National Curriculum geography and history and religious education)
- daily living skills
- physical education (including National Curriculum)
- leisure and recreation
- creative activities (including National Curriculum art and music)
- sensory exploration
- careers education including 'Insight to Work'.

We were concerned from the beginning to emphasise that the balance of activities for each individual may vary according to need, ability, interest and choice. The content of the curriculum will 'vary from one pupil to another and for the same pupil over time, in response to changing needs.' (Sebba, Byers and Rose, 1993). Students are entitled to a broad curriculum, made appropriate to their needs through a variety of teaching styles.

The content for each curriculum area was determined by consulting National Curriculum documentation and by brainstorming. For example, careers education, including 'Insight to Work' (NCC, 1990b), might include:

- work experience
- careers
- taking responsibility
- appearance
- appropriate behaviour
- keeping time
- different work environments
- co-operating and working with others

- meeting people who work in different fields
- remembering and following instructions
- industrial and commercial links
- mini-enterprise.

These lists are not exhaustive and often overlap, but provide ideas for what should and could be covered in the different curriculum areas.

We then matched the original list of entitlements to these curriculum areas to ensure that the entitlements would be met. Most entitlements were considered to be of a cross-curricular nature and not identified with one particular curriculum area. These entitlements (for example, problem solving, equality of opportunity, political awareness) we thought should be of importance in day to day practice and should be highlighted across the range of learning situations. Other entitlements were more obviously aligned with curriculum areas (for example, numeracy with mathematics and daily living skills).

Rationale

As a team we developed an overall rationale for the seniors curriculum, expanding both the school and departmental philosophy and aims and stressing the basis of entitlement (see figure 2.1 and chapter 12).

Each member of staff then took a different curriculum area and wrote a draft rationale, often referring to National Curriculum or local education authority documentation. These were discussed at meetings, many alterations were made and statements streamlined. A rationale for each area was agreed. This process of discussion was important for sharing beliefs and ideas, helping us to work together and develop a common sense of purpose. The rationales generally consist of a few sentences explaining why that curriculum area is important to students in the seniors department and outlining the aims. Figure 2.2 shows an example.

We produced a written document at this stage for members of staff throughout the school detailing curriculum areas, rationales and content for the senior department curriculum as agreed at that time.

Student curriculum guide

In addition to this curriculum documentation, students have been involved in the production of a separate curriculum guide which they developed and designed to describe learning activities in the seniors department. The curriculum guide was produced at HYTEC

20

The philosophy of the seniors curriculum is fundamentally the same as for all students in education; to maximise personal potential by offering a curriculum which is characterised by breadth, balance, relevance, differentiation, progression and continuity; and to prepare the individual for the opportunities, choices, responsibilities and experiences of adult life.

We aim to offer a broad, balanced and appropriate curriculum, meeting individual needs within a wide range of entitlements. The curriculum is based on entitlement and the right of every young person to participate fully in a variety of learning experiences and activities. Curriculum content and approaches to learning must be flexible to provide equality of opportunity and access, by recognising diverse needs.

We aim to create an environment where students are valued and respected and where staff and students work in a productive and co-operative atmosphere. Central to this ethos is an emphasis on the rights and responsibilities of individuals, particularly in determining their own lives. This is facilitated by promoting self advocacy, offering choices and encouraging decision making. We aim to offer learning opportunities where self-reliance, use of initiative and personal responsibility are emphasised. Students are involved in planning and reviewing their own experiences and achievements.

The seniors curriculum complements and builds on the primary and middle school curriculum and incorporates the national curriculum. It provides a transition between school and the community, aiming to realistically prepare students for their adult life. This involves the provision of opportunities for integration with other schools, colleges, work environments and the community in general.

The seniors curriculum is not static but will continue to evolve and be evaluated.

Figure 2.1: Curriculum rationale

Sensory Exploration Rationale.

Our capacity to learn is dependent on our ability to perceive through the five senses; smell, hearing, taste, touch and sight. By utilising the senses we can gain information about our environment. We recognise the right of all pupils to learn and explore through multi-sensory activities throughout the school day. We aim to provide challenging learning experiences, using technology where appropriate, which encourage the young people to be in control of their environment. Through sensory exploration we aim to encourage choice, stimulation, relaxation and opportunities to

---

Figure 2.2: Sensory exploration rationale

(Hertfordshire Youth Technology and Enterprise Centre, a local education authority funded curriculum centre) by twelve students from the seniors department during a work experience placement. This guide incorporates students' comments, symbols, pictures and photographs (figure 2.3).

Monitoring

The curriculum document should not be a static reference document removed from the reality of classroom teaching. We matched the curriculum document to the senior department timetable to ensure that, as a department, we were covering all identified curriculum areas. Any areas which were not being covered on the timetable could then be noted and included in future planning.

It is also necessary to carry out curriculum audits for individual students, comparing the planned senior department curriculum with the received classroom curriculum and the needs of the student. As noted by Sebba, Byers and Rose (1993) and NCC (1992a and 1992b) it is important to conduct an audit of the received curriculum rather than the students' timetable to identify actual learning opportunities (see chapter 4). Again, this will assist future planning.

Implications

In this section we highlight a number of underlying issues which need further thought and discussion in the ongoing development of the seniors curriculum and accompanying documentation.

It's good for you.

It's good to have hobbies
you can learn from reading books.
Learning to take turns
Finding things to do with your Spare time at
Breaktime,Lunchtime
Relax and enjoy it- it' s friendly.

Things we do.

Basketball

Football

Running

Cycling

Cricket

Keep fit

CHAT TO FRIENDS
Drawing
Reading
Making drinks
Snooker
Listen to music
Play games on computers

Figure 2.3: Leisure and recreation

Meeting the needs of all students

The philosophy of the school is reflected in the entitlement of all students to a broad, balanced and relevant curriculum. We discussed how the framework should allow for individual needs whilst ensuring this entitlement. All students should be involved in appropriate learning experiences with their peers, whether in their own school, mainstream or college provision.

The curriculum document may be seen as a vehicle to promote breadth, balance and relevance. It then lies with the staff to differentiate the curriculum activities to ensure access.

The process of curriculum development evoked discussion about how, through student decision making, varied teaching and learning styles and resource management, access could be promoted. We do, however, recognise that organisational factors can cause limitations to curriculum access.

Class and individual timetables are not generally organised in terms of curriculum activities. Many activities, such as the Duke of Edinburgh's award scheme, further education link courses, the Diploma of Vocational Education and links with a local farm are cross-curricular. There is then sometimes confusion between the cross-curricular approach and the curriculum areas as defined and used for summative recording purposes.

One way forward may be to utilise an approach where each series of lessons can be planned to be subject focused or referenced to different curriculum areas as appropriate. This would also assist in monitoring curriculum coverage. A possible means of recording this is illustrated in figure 2.4.

Pupil involvement

The need to involve students in curriculum decisions, whilst implicit in the overall seniors curriculum rationale, will need to be made explicit within the document. Students should have curriculum choices within the timetable to reflect their own interests and should be consulted as part of the annual review procedure with regard to their future needs and wishes. Students should also be involved in recording and evaluation, particularly through Record of Achievement procedures (see chapter 11).

It will be necessary to discuss and illustrate ways of promoting pupil involvement, especially for those students with profound and multiple learning difficulties. For example, the student curriculum guide can be

DUKE OF EDINBURGH'S AWARD SCHEME: GREEN CLUB.

ACTIVITIES.	CURRICULUM AREAS.
Group discussion to decide focus of work, environmental issues.	Communication.
Familiarisation of environmental issues, videos, magazines, letters.	Science - Life and Living processes; Geography - Environmental; Communication; Information Technology.
Group discussion to decide format of Green Club.	Communication.
Marketing the Green Club, design and production of posters, logo, questionnaires, interviews, membership pack (designing. and making badges, fact sheet, book mark, membership card.)	Technology - Designing and Making; Mathematics - Measuring.
Advertising the Green Club, presentation launch in assembly, canvassing for membership, compiling list and working out quantities.	Communication; Mathematics - Number.
Issuing packs.	
Expanding Green Club outside school, letters.	Communication

Figure 2.4: Example of Duke of Edinburgh's award scheme sheet

used as an introduction into the seniors department ᴇ choice and understanding.

Record keeping

As a comprehensive planning, recording and monitoring system is developed for the department it will be necessary to describe that process within the curriculum document (see chapter 10). The system needs to:

- be developed and agreed by staff in the department;
- monitor an individual student's curriculum coverage over time to ensure breadth and balance;
- monitor an individual student's progress in relation to priorities identified in the annual review procedure;
- address the issue of matching the cross-curricular approach with curriculum areas (see figure 2.4);
- enable class teachers to keep track of students in their class whilst these students are participating in a number of activities with different staff;
- include student self evaluation and recording;
- link with the Record of Achievement process.

Age appropriateness

We are concerned to ensure that the curriculum offered is appropriate to the age of the students without compromising activities which are necessary and relevant to individual pupils. These two demands are sometimes in conflict. For example, use of information technology may be need-relevant and enhance choice and decision making without compromising the issue of age appropriateness. Communication activities based on early interactions between infant and caregiver (Nind and Hewett, 1988) may be necessary and relevant for some students with profound and multiple learning difficulties (see chapter 7) but may not be considered age appropriate. This clearly poses a dilemma.

Sharing professional expertise

We would like to involve a wider variety of contributors, for example careers advisory staff, further education college lecturers, physiotherapists, governors and parents in order to utilise the experience, interests and expertise of others. This could be facilitated by distributing the

. ınnutes of curriculum development meetings to the above groups of people. There may also be opportunities where aspects of curriculum development could more formally be addressed, for example at parent consultations or careers meetings (see chapter 6).

Curriculum content

The content of the curriculum areas needs to be structured in some way to ensure continuity and progression rather than being a pot pourri of activities and experiences. This will be carried out by referring to subject co-ordinators within school, National Curriculum and local education authority documentation where appropriate.

Conclusion

The process of curriculum development is on-going. In this chapter we have described part of this process for a department in one school. In many ways we have been fortunate in that, owing to amalgamation issues, development has been gradual. This has enabled us to develop as a team.

It is important that curriculum development is not seen as a separate theoretical process carried out in meetings but is evident in the class-room. It must continue to reflect classroom practice and maintain the flexibility to encompass new activities and courses, whilst allowing for the diversity of student and staff needs.

It is also important to keep up to date with mainstream developments and to collaborate with staff from other provision for pupils with learning difficulties.

To ensure progression it will be necessary to review both the curriculum in practice and curriculum documentation on a regular basis.

Chapter Three

*Personal and Social Education in a School
for Pupils with Severe Learning Difficulties*
Will Fletcher and Judith Gordon

Introduction

Prior to the introduction of the Education Reform Act (ERA) (DES, 1988) and to the implementation of the National Curriculum in special schools, there appeared to be something of a 'knee jerk reaction' (Ainscow, 1988) to some of the anticipated proposals. There certainly seemed to be a fear that personal and social development was in danger of being under-represented or subordinated to an inferior position within the curriculum. However, it is possible that many of the traditional approaches under the banner of personal and social education (PSE) were conceived of in somewhat narrow and limited ways. Programmes were often delivered through the teaching of specific 'self-help' or independence skills, such as personal hygiene, dressing and the tying of shoe laces, sometimes without regard to the context in which such activities usually take place. The ultimate goal of such activities appeared to be more concerned with 'social acceptability' or 'vocational adaptability' than with empowerment and personal autonomy. There is clearly, however, a need to recognise that a relationship exists between these models which are frequently portrayed as being incompatible. A knowledge of the demands, norms and expectations of society will be an important element in preparing young people for the opportunities, responsibilities and experiences of adult life (see chapter 2).

Carpenter (1992) suggests that goals concerned with practical independence and self-help skills should be retained but extended to offer the opportunity of maximum personal autonomy.

Sebba, Byers and Rose (1993) state the need for a distinction to be made between personal and social development and traditional courses of personal and social education - the two are not necessarily synonymous. Discrete courses of personal and social education may contribute only partially to pupils' personal and social development. The suggestion is made that

> pupil's personal and social development will be enhanced by increased access to the whole curriculum on a number of different levels. (p.75)

Within the programmes of study for the core and other foundation subjects of the National Curriculum and in various curriculum guidance documents, references are made to pupil participation, initiation, expressing opinions and making choices on equal terms with teachers and other pupils. There appears to be a good deal of emphasis placed upon active learning and involvement in decision making, including the recognition that involving pupils in self assessment helps pupils to a better understanding of their own strengths and needs. These aspects of the basic curriculum are particularly important for pupils who have often in the past been offered a more passive role in their learning as characterised by Ryder and Campbell's (1988) medical/transitional model. Nevertheless, despite the relevance of a more student centred approach in promoting personal and social development, it is often through the 'intangibles which come from the spirit and ethos of each school' (NCC, 1990a) that the most powerful messages come.

What is adulthood?

The authors have a particular responsibility for the education of 16 to 19 year old students within a school for pupils with severe learning difficulties and therefore the idea of preparing students for the opportunities, responsibilities and experiences of adult life has a particular and immediate significance for us. It seemed important to put our curriculum to the test and ascertain what messages about adulthood had been received to date (see chapter 4).

A group of six students were asked a number of questions through an informal discussion. Their responses were both informative and disturbing.

Question: What is an adult?

'when you are 18'
'being grown-up and mature'

'you behave - mature and very good like adults'
'they are independent'
'go to work'
'do what you like'
'adults sit with their arms folded and shut up'
'be mature and behave.'

There were varying degrees of agreement and dissension to some of these ideas. We probed a little further.

Question: How do you think adults behave?

'mature'
'sometimes good sometimes bad'
'they do as they're told.'

Question: Is being an adult to do with behaviour or age?

All but one student thought it was to do with how old you were, though not with any great conviction.

The exercise was clearly not easy for the students and it was difficult to determine whether or not the students were giving the answer they thought we wanted to hear. Either way it served to highlight a clear tendency to view adulthood as something that is earned by virtue of 'good behaviour' rather than a physical and legal fact.

We became aware of how easy it was to reinforce this view of adulthood by the kinds of language used in a variety of contexts.

In *Young People With Handicaps: the Road to Adulthood* (OECD/CERI, 1986) it is argued that the main indicators of adulthood are:

- Personal autonomy, independence and adult status;
- Productive activity (i.e., 'working life') leading to economic self-sufficiency;
- Social interaction, community participation, leisure and recreation;
- Roles within the family. (p. 7)

This study argues that most aspects of adulthood in our society are earned and are dependent upon achieving a level of skills in these areas and also dependent upon other people acknowledging the fact. This then places students with a severe disability at a considerable disadvantage in achieving adult status.

The authors believe that adult status should be automatically conferred on young people irrespective of the degree to which 'indications' may be achieved. A detailed discussion of personal autonomy as an educational aim is beyond the scope of this chapter. Nevertheless it is important to acknowledge some possible difficulties.

The aim of personal autonomy may not be shared by some parents thus giving rise to potential conflict as students become more assertive. Discussion and sensitive consideration of the issues involved may, under certain circumstances, help to resolve such conflict. However, in some cultures autonomy is not considered a desirable aim, particularly for women. Careful planning must ensure that the content of course work is genuinely realistic and in the best interests of the students to whom we believe staff owe a primary duty.

The notion of autonomy and adult status for students with profound and multiple learning difficulties requires an interpretation of the curriculum which avoids tokenism yet which is consistent with the aim of empowerment in as many aspects of their lives as possible. Learners who may not achieve the main indicators of adulthood referred to earlier, nevertheless have the right to the dignity and status accorded to others of a similar age. For students to take on increased responsibility for their own actions and learning there needs to be a deliberate and implicit expectation on the part of the teacher that this should occur. It requires of teachers that they devolve some of their control over the content and delivery of the curriculum to the students through a more negotiated approach to teaching. It seems unrealistic to expect students to be able to exercise choice and decision making without creating the conditions in which they can feel empowered to do so effectively. This empowerment of students is enhanced by the development of confidence and self-esteem which comes from the knowledge that views, choices and decisions will be respected, valued and acted upon (see chapter 12).

It seemed necessary to re-examine the whole curriculum in order that the practical day-to-day content matched up to the rhetoric of the various policy documents.

Informal discussions with the staff in the further education department seemed to highlight a number of particularly important areas for consideration:

- relationships between staff and students;
- opportunities for choice and decision making, including active participation and negotiation of learning priorities;
- specific content of discrete courses such as health and sex education;
- continuity of approach between school and home;
- school rules;
- opportunities for careers education, work experience and community participation;

- ensuring a shared philosophy or consistent approach across all members of staff.

In examining some of these areas it became clear that many of the issues raised were not specific to older pupils. On the contrary, they required discussion across the whole school. It was also clear that personal and social education could not be successfully delivered without establishing a common consensus among all members of school staff throughout the whole curriculum (see chapter 6). Pupils' entitlement to personal and social education from five to sixteen must be the concern and responsibility of the whole staff team. In the next section of this chapter we have included an example of one attempt to establish a set of agreed principles for working with pupils of all ages.

Raising issues

'But why do I have periods?'

This was a question posed by a young woman of seventeen, which, together with other similar questions, might pose a considerable challenge to staff working in an environment which is not supportive enough to look at this issue with sensitivity. In the authors' experience, young women with severe learning difficulties are unlikely to be deemed by society to have the necessary skills to be adequate parents. If society will not accept this level of personal autonomy, it is important that the reasons for this are clearly elaborated and understood by students. The delivery of the more personal and sexual aspects of the personal and social education curriculum for students with learning difficulties is a minefield of moral dilemmas. Young people with severe learning difficulties often lead highly supervised lives. They are more dependent for their freedom of social and sexual expression on parents and carers than other young people of a similar age. Nevertheless the authors believe that students should not be denied access to a comprehensive sex education programme.

In an attempt to negotiate the minefield we set up a weekly discrete personal and social education group with students between sixteen and nineteen from our all age school for pupils with severe learning difficulties. The school had recently taken the decision not to have a separate department for those pupils with profound and multiple learning difficulties. All pupils were to be educated within their appropriate age group - a move which was generally welcomed, but which increased the problems of effectively differentiating in all areas of the curriculum without providing some discrete sessions.

The general criterion for inclusion within the group was that each student should be verbally communicative and either able, or in our opinion potentially able, to work co-operatively in a group. We did not intend to be over tokenistic by including those with complex learning difficulties in this group. The authors acknowledge the possible dangers of denying access to those who might benefit from a particular course. Nevertheless, we found it difficult at this stage to conceive of a programme that was not substantially dependent on language, role play and discussion for its delivery.

The issue of providing opportunities for personal and social education for students with profound and multiple learning difficulties may, to some extent, reside with the attitudes of staff towards an individual's privacy and dignity. As previously stated, adult status does not have to be earned. However, personal and social education which relies solely upon verbal discussion and written material clearly limits access to all but a relatively small number of students. There is now a task for the staff team to develop means of ensuring the widest possible access to such materials through the appropriate use of symbols, photographs, video and other augmentative methods whilst guarding against a tokenistic approach to complicated issues (see chapter 7).

We accepted at the outset that the weekly personal and social education group would constitute only a part of the personal and social education curriculum for those in the group. Although the group met at the same time and in the same place each week, we intended the sessions to be flexible in approach and teaching styles and open to review and adjustment of content and delivery. Initially, the specific aims of the sessions were to provide a safe and trustful environment in which to discuss, share, impart knowledge of a personal or confidential nature and positively to build on and enhance social development. If we were to begin to help our students to become aware of and comfortable with their adult bodies, and to explore issues surrounding adulthood, adult sexuality, emotions, relationships and so on, it was, we felt, very important to create an environment where the students could be empowered to take as active a part in their learning as possible.

We intended to use an approach based on negotiation to facilitate learning - an approach in which self advocacy was strongly encouraged (see chapter 12). There was a deliberate attempt to move away from the medical/transitional model. We hoped that the students with whom we proposed to work would have something to teach us, even if only that we were getting it wrong.

Issues of confidentiality were clarified very early on in the sessions. Barring information which we, as professionals, had to pass on, specifics discussed or personal comments made were to be confidential. The word 'private' was used alongside the new term 'confidential' in this instance. A notice stating 'PSE, please do not disturb' was produced by the students to be placed on the door for each session. We decided to use *Living Your Life* (Craft, 1991), a recently developed personal and social education package, as a core of our personal and social education curriculum. As time went on we supplemented this with our own and other resources where we felt it to be necessary. The group spent quite some time on group-building exercises at the outset to build trust and develop group cohesion. During these early sessions 'PSE group rules' were developed. These were brainstormed and refined by the students in negotiation with the staff. Such details as a specific procedure for dealing with constant interruptions were included in the rules as well as clarification of where and when the group sessions would take place. Group rules also tackled issues such as turn-taking, listening and valuing others' contributions. This reflected the way in which we hoped the group would work, building self-esteem and bringing the young people together to learn from themselves and from one another as well as from us. Most young people in schools for pupils with severe learning difficulties find it far more difficult to interact with one another than with the adults around them and this means that peer-group modelling - so vital to young people in their initiations into adulthood - is often not present at all or is not very powerful. The group sessions could be seen as a way of enhancing these elements.

The current situation

The personal and social education group has been running for over a year now. Group members have left the school and others have moved into the further education classes. Staff working with the group have remained stable. During this time there have been successes and failures, serious moments, sad moments and quite a lot of fun. A few weeks after the start of sessions on emotions we learned of the death of a popular escort on one of the school buses. The students who knew her well were clearly upset. We felt it necessary to devote the afternoon to a discussion around the issues of death and loss. One student, who generally made very little contribution to group discussions, suddenly surprised everybody by expressing at great length, and with great depth of feeling and sensitivity, her thoughts about death and mourning.

Although it may seem obvious, this reminded us of the importance of allowing students the time to express themselves, particularly on difficult issues from which there can be a temptation to over protect and shelter. It was also brought home to us that it was both acceptable and right for staff to express and admit to their own feelings. Presenting life in simple, uncomplicated 'happy ever after' scenarios is both unrealistic and unhelpful. Students often have more knowledge and insight than they are given credit for.

Differentiation is a constant challenge. During one exercise which involved passing around a mirror and commenting on emotions and facial expressions, one student studied himself in the mirror and commented: 'penis'. It was a word which had been introduced recently and one which he was aware had been greeted with approval when used in the right context. Until then we had not fully realised how much the students were still entrenched in the 'giving teacher what he wants' scenario and this was a timely reminder to exercise a more incisive approach to our planning and evaluating. When, for example, an exercise works well for some of the group, it is very important to clarify aims and make objective judgements about its validity. Formal evaluations at the conclusion of modules and regular feedback sessions with small groups and individual students here become indispensable to planning course content. During a recent evaluation session a male student who had taken a particular interest in physical changes occurring during puberty asked if we could: 'do some more stuff on sex please'.

Recently a member of staff not working with the group asked to be informed about the subject matter of the sessions - she had students in her class who were working on areas of personal and social education and she was unable to follow them up. This we realised should have been built in from the outset. Comments gleaned recently from students in answer to the question 'what is PSE?' include:

'writing on the board'
'frightening things'
'happy things'
'doing the tape'
'hygiene and keeping clean'
'inside us - how you feel'

and perhaps the most honest and maybe most profound:

'I can't explain it'.

There are pitfalls in attempting to move away from a prescriptive approach to teaching and adopting an open-ended approach. This can be empowering for students, but may be seen as disempowering for staff. It is a juggling act to put equal value on all contributions whilst trying to focus on issues which are fundamental to the curriculum and at the same time empowering students to go some way towards setting their own agenda.

Individual concerns which have been picked up during group sessions are being followed up in one to one weekly tutorial sessions to which all students have access. Nevertheless there is a danger of regarding an intensive discrete session such as this as covering the personal and social education curriculum. It should more properly be seen as just one component of an overall approach to working towards personal and social development for all.

Back to first principles

It is claimed that access to a curriculum which includes programmes of personal and social education is an entitlement for all pupils from 5 to 16 (NCC, 1990a) and that:

> Schools therefore need to consider creating policy statements and related schemes of work which will enable them to implement such programmes (Sebba, Byers, Rose, 1993, p. 76).

As previously indicated, however, promoting personal and social education is a matter for the whole curriculum. It seemed important, therefore, to establish an agreed set of principles to which all staff would strive to adhere. A number of workshops were set up to discuss issues of common concern. The statement outlined in figure 3.1 is the result of these discussions.

The process of drawing up staff principles has heightened staff awareness of the need to adjust teaching styles to accommodate the ethos embodied in the statement.

Such a statement may begin to help staff to ensure that more aspects of personal and social development are addressed. Meanwhile a personal and social education working party has been established with the aims of: exploring present provision and approaches to personal and social education throughout the school; addressing specific content issues and providing continuity and progression; formulating a collaborative working policy for personal and social education.

STAFF PRINCIPLES
We the staff agree to abide by the following principles:

INDIVIDUALITY
1) To respect pupils' individuality: concentration span
                                            development level
                                            time to act/respond
                                            interests.
2) To respect pupils' privacy.
3) To address pupils by name.
4) To facilitate the development of personal autonomy.

COMMUNICATION
1) To communicate with pupils in the most appropriate mode.
2) To speak to, and not at.
3) To respect the pupils' right of choice.
4) To show sensitivity in use of voice tone and intonation.

ERGONOMICS and MOBILITY
1) To respect the right to mobility.
2) Pupils have the right to correct furniture, and to alternative correct positioning.

SERVICES
1) To recognise a pupil's right to a broad and balanced curriculum.
2) To recognise a pupil's right to additional services as required:
        Physiotherapy
        Speech Therapy
        Occupational Therapy
        Clinical Psychologist
        Educational Psychologist
        Medical
        Social Services
3) To strive for pupil representation, especially when other agencies are involved.
4) To strive to ensure pupils look forward to a fulfilling post-school future.

Figure 3.1: Staff principles

Conclusion

In our experience, parents have responded very positively to our attempts to deliver a more comprehensive personal and social education curriculum. New issues are now being actively raised at home by the students. This has been reflected in discussions at annual review meetings, which are often more open as a result. Liaison also takes place on a regular basis through home-school books or discussion with parents.

However, we are aware that we have been unable to convey fully our philosophy and approach to the parent body as a whole. The school's Governing Body has expressed support for the development of a comprehensive school policy towards personal and social education and sex education. It is planned to present this policy to parents and governors at a consultation meeting in the near future. It is vital that the implementation of such a policy should be a collaborative venture between school and parents.

Whole curriculum planning for personal and social education will be a challenging and complex process but our experiences so far suggest that it will be a rewarding and worthwhile task.

Chapter Four

Beyond the Simple Audit

Sandra Galloway and David Banes

Why do schools audit?

The curriculum audit has become an accepted feature in schools throughout the country. This chapter aims to examine the value of this practice and to explore the use of the audit as part of a school's curriculum development cycle.

The staff designing the audits described in this chapter set out to analyse practice with specific aims in mind. To be of any value, such aims are usually related to school improvement and should assist the school in introducing and preparing the ground for change. The purpose of the audit process is to inform and shape that change.

The audit process

The process of conducting an audit has been well described in a range of publications (DES, 1989a; NCC, 1990a; NCC, 1992a; Sebba, Galloway and Rodbard, 1991). We do not wish to repeat all of this material. It may be useful at this point, however, to clarify two terms that we will use in this chapter:

> '*pupil shadowing*' refers to a process of intensive observation of a pupil's experiences, usually over the period of one school week;

> '*teacher audit*' refers to a process in which the teacher's perceptions of the focus of a session or activity are recorded and analysed, usually for breadth of content.

In general, the publications noted above focus upon the use of the audit as a means of monitoring breadth and balance in the curriculum. More specifically, audits are often associated with an analysis of coverage of the programmes of study for each of the National Curriculum subject areas. Such audits can take place at a variety of levels. Schools can audit the curriculum at a whole school level, at departmental level, or at the level of a single teacher.

In this chapter we will consider further aspects of practice which may usefully be investigated through an audit. These aspects include the provision of cross-curricular learning opportunities; teaching approaches and learning styles; classroom management and organisation; and the moderation of pupil achievements and teacher led assessment.

An audit of curriculum coverage

In one school, an apparently successful audit was set up in order to examine breadth of coverage of the programmes of study for information technology capability. As a result of the audit, the school was able to report that, of the five strands within technology attainment target 5, 'communicating information' was well covered, but the other four were under represented in the curriculum as currently delivered. Staff showed little surprise at this result and the most popular response was 'I could have told you that!' These people were understandably questioning what had been a complex process creating extra stress upon them and which had yielded only information that they already knew. This outcome strongly suggests that certain important questions should have been asked before starting out on the audit path - a point we shall return to at the end of this chapter.

The audit described above focused upon the National Curriculum and the monitoring of coverage in one area of the curriculum. Staff involved chose to reference activities to a pre-determined set of criteria, in this case the programmes of study for information technology capability, although the same principles would apply to any other area of the curriculum. Their aim was to make a quantitative analysis of that area of the curriculum as offered to pupils. The results for one specific pupil are presented in Figure 4.1.

These data were collected in such a way as to facilitate referencing to technology attainment target 5. They reveal that each pupil in the sample has access to microtechnology and that pupils address a range of information technology activities for a certain number of hours each week. The data may help staff to make quantitative adjustments to their practice in order to create a better balance between application of the various strands within attainment target 5. The audit results may also

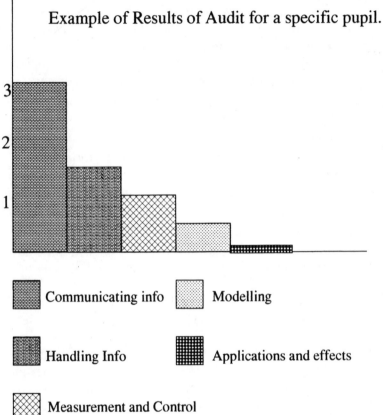

Figure 4.1: Audit results

profitably be stored in order to allow a comparison with the amount of information technology time that the same pupils are receiving after any innovations have been introduced.

It may be that information gathered for a specific purpose will not be used easily to meet other needs. However, it is appropriate to ask whether the material can realistically be put to any other use. The staff decided in this instance that they wished to go on to examine the range of teaching styles they employed in encouraging pupils to use information technology.

Auditing for change in teaching styles

The data shown in figure 4.1 are of very little value as they stand in seeking to implement a qualitative change in practice, such as the development of group work, or in an analysis of teaching styles.

There was a need, therefore, to collect a new set of raw data in order to look at the amount of time each pupil spent working in each of a predetermined set of categories for group work. Before completing any analysis, it is important that those involved in the audit process agree the criteria by which the information will be analysed. For the sake of this example, we can take the categories of:

- individual learning - by rote
- individual learning - investigations and explorations
- paired parallel activities
- co-operative activities involving the sharing of resources
- collaborative activities.

To guide those making the analysis, a number of examples of each category of activity can be given. Examples of such material can be found in the chapter on information technology in this book (see chapter 8).

The examination of a specific pupil's audit data offers figure 4.2 as an analysis of the amount of time she spent working in each of these ways. In evaluating information like this at a later date, some background on each of the pupils would be necessary in order to identify the constraints within which the staff were working. Such information could include timetables, individual objectives for the pupils involved and notes concerning the availability and organisation of relevant resources. Since this audit concerned the role of information technology across the curriculum, information was required about all those occasions in the school week when computers were available to members of staff. This was easily provided by examining class resource timetables. In more than one case, computers were classroom based all day, so it could safely be said that the computer was available for all the time that the pupils were in the room.

Examination of detailed information from the audit should also reveal occasions when using the computer might not have been appropriate. One such example may be a class activity involving cornflour painting, although even in this situation the computer might have been used effectively to assist pupils in recording the outcome.

It is also useful to re-examine background information from previous audits in order to provide guidelines for the development of a new area of the curriculum. By looking at other areas in which changes have been

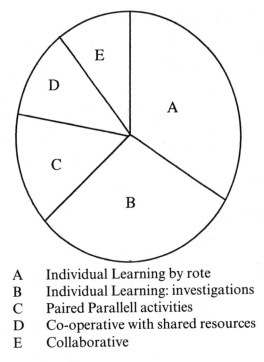

A   Individual Learning by rote
B   Individual Learning: investigations
C   Paired Parallell activities
D   Co-operative with shared resources
E   Collaborative

Figure 4.2: Group work audit

successfully implemented, it is possible to identify conditions which contributed to this success. These may include factors such as class size, the age of the pupils in the group, the range of interests and aptitudes among the pupils, and certain classroom management techniques. These conditions can then be fostered in the context of any new development such as the use of information technology in group work.

Auditing classroom management and organisation

In the following example, an audit was carried out in order to examine the management and organisation of the classroom in which a pupil with challenging behaviours had been working.

The audit was initiated as a result of the concern of a teacher regarding a pupil's seemingly inappropriate behaviour with her peers. Staff at the school felt that they had themselves developed a negative attitude towards Donna, the pupil concerned.

In this case the focus of the audit was not upon teaching activities but instead was upon the pupil's responses in a range of settings and contexts. The audit was carried out both by a shadow of the individual pupil and by a related teacher audit of the focus of the activities that were taking place. The criteria for the analysis of this audit were therefore based upon the inappropriate behaviours of the pupil. When completed, a number of issues were raised which staff could address. These were summarised in the following way:

- The inappropriate behaviours were most likely to occur in settings in which staff direction and supervision of a session were low, such as free play or drinks time.
- The behaviours were most likely to occur in the presence of pupils who had profound and multiple learning difficulties.
- Staff were responding to the behaviours in quite an aggressive manner, particularly by invading Donna's body space.

Having completed the audit, staff involved with Donna were able to make modifications to their practice.

- The timetable and the organisation of the school day were modified to reduce the number of activities in which Donna worked in unstructured settings.
- Pupil groupings were rearranged to create settings in which Donna's interactions with her peers could become more positive.
- A higher level of staff supervision was arranged for those sessions in which low structure teaching strategies and learning styles were in use.

It was possible to use the raw data gathered for this audit for a variety of other purposes after the initial analysis was completed. Notably in this case staff were able to compare the planned intention of lessons against what was actually being received by pupils. They were also able to examine the learning of more than one pupil working in the group in order to consider the ways in which classroom activities were being differentiated. This illustrates a pertinent point because the audit structure required the staff who were completing the analysis to be quite clear as to what they were looking for in terms of differentiated learning. The audit process in itself therefore helped to clarify the thinking of the staff involved as they identified the criteria by which the information was to be analysed.

The staff at this particular school have now introduced an annual audit. They intend to use this process to moderate and validate their teacher assessments of achievements within the National Curriculum. They also intend to make it possible to use the information gathered in order to analyse teaching styles and consider whether changes might contribute to improved pupil performance.

Summary

In conclusion, this chapter has suggested that auditing is a valuable process in the development of the curriculum in schools for pupils with learning difficulties. In drawing together the points regarding auditing raised in this chapter, we wish to highlight those issues which we regard as central to the auditing process.

Context issues - what additional information will be required to ensure that the audit can be analysed effectively in a variety of ways?

The use of raw audit information for a variety of purposes has a number of dangers, but if the audit is properly constructed it can be done effectively. As well as being obtained through observation or pupil shadowing, information for an audit can be gained from a number of other sources. As we have seen, these include individual and class timetables. Timetables do not always reflect the actual events of a week, however, and are often written in terms which fail to reveal the true content of lessons. Staff involved with the audit will need to be aware of this possibility and include in their planning methods of checking the validity of data based on timetables.

Staff contact rotas, lesson plans, pupil aims, schemes of work and module documentation may also prove to be significant contextual factors worthy of consideration during the audit along with information about the availability of resources and staff expertise in using equipment. This sort of information can be put together in an audit package which will ultimately also include data from pupil shadows and teacher audit.

Sample issues - how will decisions be made about who to audit?

The focus of an audit is often upon the experiences of individual pupils. In order to be of most value in whole school development it is important that a sample across a number of pupils is taken and that these pupils can be seen as representative of a wider school population.

For example, in one audit the school particularly chose pupils who could be referred to as having challenging behaviours, as having profound and multiple learning difficulties or as having severe learning difficulties and then generalised from the experiences of these key pupils.

Analysis issues - how will the criteria for the audit be established?

Possibly the most important features of an effective audit are the criteria by which the raw information is analysed. The criteria must be clear enough so that an outsider could conduct the analysis if necessary. In the examples discussed above, clear criteria can be discerned, including the National Curriculum programmes of study, preset goals and objectives for individual pupils, a range of criteria agreed by staff when examining groupwork and a set of distinct behaviours exhibited by a single pupil.

A number of other possibilities exist. The aims and objectives established for an individual pupil often provide a viable starting point, particularly where a pupil shadow technique is to be used. Are the aims and objectives being met? Are skills being generalised into situations other than those provided in direct teaching sessions? Is there a consistency of approach and management to avoid confusion?

Staff conducting an audit of curriculum coverage may wish to consider such aspects as the restrictions imposed upon a particular pupil's curriculum by problems of access. In some instances staff may be more concerned to record pupil interactions or to analyse situations which provide opportunities to develop or build upon specific skills in a range of contexts across the curriculum. This may lead to the involvement of support staff and therapists so that the audit will begin to examine the working of the multidisciplinary team at the school.

Whatever criteria are established, they must be clear to all involved in the auditing process. Operating in a well defined and focused way will enable staff to make effective use of their time during the auditing process and will prevent the collection of superfluous data. It is undoubtedly better to conduct an audit based upon limited criteria than to attempt to address a broad range of issues all at once.

Development issues - how will the staff of the school use the information gained through an audit to inform future planning?

There is no purpose in conducting an audit unless it is to be acted upon. An effective audit will identify areas of strength and provide clear indications of areas which will require further development. The analysis of this information will allow staff to decide whether pupils' needs are being met consistently. It should suggest areas in which problems lie, whether these are to do with resourcing, staff expertise, organisational issues or the effectiveness of the multidisciplinary team. The audit may also suggest those areas of the curriculum that are best taught as discrete areas by the professionals involved.

Such information should be used to inform the staff development programme of the whole school. But before embarking upon a course of action following the audit, staff should construct a careful plan. What are the implications for timetable management of any action to be taken? Is there a resourcing issue or a need for staff development? Such questions should assist staff in considering the way forward to providing a well planned, relevant, balanced and broad curriculum for all pupils.

In conclusion, it is our belief that the best way to ensure that an audit is worthwhile, is to plan effectively the wider context in which the audit is functioning.

- Is the audit related to an area of the schools' development plan?
- Is the audit likely to tell us anything new?
- Are we committed to act upon the results of this audit?

If we can respond positively to each of these questions then the audit process will be a valuable one. However, there is a danger that schools may conduct an audit of a curricular area, and then find too many frustrations implicit in the process to take that audit further. What then needs to be ensured is that a more open and imaginative use of the audit tool is made. In such cases auditing can be a powerful vehicle for encouraging whole school development in many areas.

49

Chapter Five

A Modular Approach to the Curriculum for Pupils with Learning Difficulties

Richard Rose

The author wishes to acknowledge the work of staff at Wren Spinney School, Kettering, all of whom have contributed to the development of the ideas here presented.

An examination of the organisation and management of the curriculum in schools for pupils with learning difficulties, suggests that many of the problems being confronted by staff on a daily basis are common across these schools. This was certainly evidenced by the requests made to the National Curriculum Development Team based at the University of Cambridge Institute of Education during the early stages of the introduction of the National Curriculum. Issues related to time management, curriculum referencing, differentiation and recording were raised in all schools, and continue to cause difficulties in many. Whilst some schools have successfully tackled some of these problems, many still recognise that there is a considerable way to travel before the broad, balanced and relevant curriculum for which all teachers are striving is achieved. This chapter will consider one method by which a school has attempted to address several of the curriculum management issues which have traditionally proved troublesome.

In *Redefining the Whole Curriculum for Pupils with Learning Difficulties* (1993) Sebba, Byers and Rose emphasised the need for a whole school approach to curriculum planning. In so doing they were aware that pressure of time and the weight of demands made upon schools could lead to an unhealthy cutting of corners.

If this statement is true of schools as a whole, it is equally applicable to staff charged with the responsibility for delivering the curriculum. Recent years have seen increased pressures upon staff in schools, with the introduction of new initiatives such as the National Curriculum and its associated testing and assessment procedures, teacher appraisal, the Technical and Vocational Education Initiative, and Records of Achievement procedures all making major demands upon teacher time. Of all the new requirements, it is those most closely associated with the curriculum which have been the focus of attention in most schools. The National Curriculum has led teachers to ask many questions mostly centred upon three words which have been at the heart of the National Curriculum debate for all schools, but which have been seen to have a particular pertinence in schools for pupils with learning difficulties. These three words are, of course, breadth, balance and relevance.

Curriculum review

In order to address concerns regarding breadth, balance and relevance in the curriculum provided for its pupils with a wide range of learning difficulties, Wren Spinney School has recently reviewed its curriculum policies and content. This has involved the whole of the school staff in an examination of the school's central aims, and in a process of curriculum development which sets out to ensure that the needs of all individuals within the school community are being met.

As part of this process, staff at Wren Spinney School have, in recent years, developed a series of curriculum modules. These are in effect short courses, often, though not always, with a subject focus, specifically designed for use with particular groups of pupils.

The origins of these modules can be traced to a period in the school's history when an evaluation project examined the effectiveness of teaching methods being deployed in the school (Newman and Rose, 1990). Concerns were expressed at this time that the balance of the curriculum provided for some pupils in school required attention. It became apparent, for example, that some pupils were spending a considerable amount of time working in certain curriculum areas, physical education for example, and very little time was given to others, such as science or technology. Further examination indicated that whilst some aspects of this imbalance could be related to individual pupils, there was also a general lack of breadth which needed to be addressed. In common with many schools for pupils with learning difficulties, a great deal of consideration had been given to the personal and social needs of pupils. Similarly, the physical needs of pupils, and in particular those with profound and multiple learning difficulties, were being adequately addressed. Other areas appeared to be greatly influenced by teacher expertise or interest. For example, those pupils fortunate enough to have a musical teacher often received a considerable amount of music on their timetable, whereas other pupils, possibly even in the next class, received little or no music.

The evaluation project established at the school began by addressing the issues of breadth and balance whilst also taking account of the need to increase staff expertise by a sharing of experiences. As a first step in this process, a short course in science was introduced to pupils for whom this was quite a novel experience. The lessons, taught for the most part by teachers with very little experience of science teaching, were recorded on video and discussed at length. Pupils' responses were recorded, as were teachers' reactions to this new initiative (as reported by Newman and Rose, 1990). It became apparent that not only did the pupils enjoy and respond to the science activities presented, but that the staff also perceived in this experiment an opportunity to develop their own teaching ideas, and to confront some of the curriculum management issues, such as planning and recording, which were apparent within the school.

Following the success of the science course, further short courses were developed in other curriculum areas, focusing upon those in which we had identified shortcomings. Within school, a cascade approach to professional development, in which teachers, having developed courses, worked with others who had not, ensured that by the end of a year all staff in school had gained experience of developing, teaching and evaluating a short course. Team teaching was developed in which teachers who had gained experience in delivering courses worked alongside those who had not. This approach encouraged evaluation, promoted the sharing of ideas, and provided on site, in-service training directly related to the pupils with whom staff were working. Further to this, a format was developed which was used consistently through these courses, and ensured that staff with little expertise in a subject area could pick up a relevant course book and teach from it. This did not preclude teachers contributing their own materials and ideas, which could be added to the course and increase its value as a teaching resource.

One of the greatest advantages of working in this way was that the staff as a whole had addressed some of the curriculum areas perceived as being weak within the school. This increased staff awareness in specific curriculum areas and began to redress the balance and breadth problems which had been identified through the process of review.

National Curriculum influence

The introduction of the National Curriculum brought a further series of challenges to the school. The development of short courses with a specific focus had enabled staff to broaden the curriculum on offer to pupils, yet this still lacked a certain cohesion. Often staff were developing courses which, whilst wholly relevant to the pupils targetted, were still unrelated to other curricular activities within the school. In many ways the National Curriculum became an ally by assisting staff at the school to focus upon specific groups of programmes of study when developing courses. The new impetus which the National Curriculum gave to curriculum development in school was supported by the earlier work in course development which had taken place. A culture of curriculum development was established, and this assisted when addressing the introduction of the National Curriculum.

What had started out as short courses, gradually evolved to become curriculum modules with a set format (see figure 5.1 below). This format was designed to have several advantages for classroom staff who needed a logical progression through the curriculum. These included the listing of required resources, the provision of lesson outlines and the clarification of curriculum references. Most of the modules now in use take the form of a five or ten week course which allows them to be taught either over a half term or a full term.

The importance of clear policy and curriculum planning

Curriculum modules, whilst having many advantages which will be discussed in this chapter, have limited use unless they form part of a planning process based upon clear policy. The involvement of all staff in the development of policy is essential if it is to be effectively implemented and managed with any enthusiasm (Bignell, 1991; Lacey, Smith and Tilstone, 1991; Sebba, Byers and Rose, 1993).

When Wren Spinney embarked upon the implementation of curriculum modules, many were developed in isolation from an overall curriculum plan. The initial advantages which these modules provided,

Example from Curriculum Module : LEARNING ABOUT MAPS

Lesson 7

This lesson should build upon work from the previous lesson, encouraging pupils to see signs and symbols as respresenting real places on maps.

Equipment

A selection of maps. Ordnance survey maps with plastic covers. Mapboards. A selection of art and craft materials Map symbol cards, OHP pens, Computer with mouse, and "Paintspa" software.

Activity 1

Begin as in the previous lesson by looking at symbols on maps. Encourage pupils to go around the school looking for signs and symbols. Provide them with signs and symbols which match those around the school.

Use the mapboards. Pupils should, depending upon their need, be encouraged to match either the squares of the map, or match the symbols to the pictures on the map. (e.g. picture of the church to the symbol.)

Using sections from real O.S. sheets and plastic covers, get pupils to mark some of the symbols which they have learned using the OHP pens.

Activity 2

Encourage pupils to make a sign or symbol for their classroom or for another place of their choice. Talk to them about what this might represent, maybe the people in the class, or the activities which take place within it. Pupils should be encouraged to make their own design and to choose the way they want to make it, and the materials they wish to use. Talk to them about possibly making a collage, or painting, or using the computer, or even a combination of these.

Curriculum references - Geography.

Extract information from and add it to pictorial maps.
Examine pictures and pictorial maps.

SEE CROSS REFERENCES TO OTHER CURRICULUM AREAS AT THE BACK OF THIS MODULE

Figure 5.1: Module format

mainly those of thorough preparation, resource and time management and assistance with recording, were somewhat dissipated by a lack of structure. As curriculum policy has been more clearly defined, it has become easier to see how curriculum modules can be used to a fuller advantage. In order to illustrate this, examples are given here from the school science policy document.

The model (figure 5.2) shows the cycle of science focused topics to be followed by pupils in the senior department of Wren Spinney School.

In year A, the pupils follow four courses in science. One of these is called 'Collecting from Nature'. Within this particular area several modules may be available for staff to use with pupils (as illustrated in the model). The ones used will depend upon the needs of the pupils, the preferences of staff, and the work which has been undertaken with the pupils in the past. The model provided ensures that pupils receive a breadth of science experiences. After three years pupils will have progressed through years A, B, and C. The cycle then begins again, and pupils will receive work from different modules which will reinforce a familiar curriculum area, such as 'Collecting from Nature', but providing a different content and using different modules.

The advantages of curriculum modules

What then are the advantages of using curriculum modules in a school for pupils with learning difficulties ? It has to be said that many of the advantages which have been experienced are those which favour staff as much as pupils. As was stated earlier in this chapter, the weight of demands, and the pressure of time upon staff in schools is immense. Any system which is implemented must, therefore, be seen to support staff in the management of time and in clarifying a route for curriculum delivery, rather than adding an extra burden to the workload.

Management of time

Concern was often expressed that examples of good practice within school were seldom shared, and that successful lessons and teaching approaches were being lost. Whilst occasional efforts were made to disseminate good practice from the classroom through staff meetings and training days, it was often true to say that staff who were preparing and teaching, for example, effective mathematics lessons, rarely had an opportunity to share this with others. The written curriculum modules ensured that the content of lessons was not lost. Similarly, the modules enabled other staff to see methods of deployment which had been used successfully by colleagues. By developing this approach, initially demanding upon staff time, there was considerable overall advantage in time management as the modules can be used again at a different time by different staff with new pupils, with much of the preparation having been completed. A set format also saved staff time and ensured that

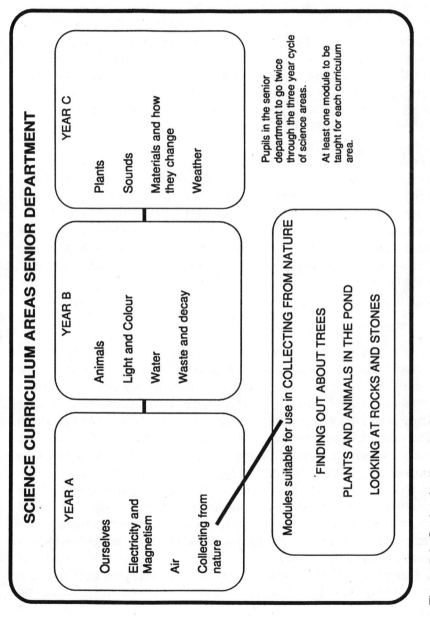

Figure 5.2: Cycle of science topics

when staff were released from class to work on module development they could progress quickly without having to spend time working on layout or content headings.

Management of resources

By listing equipment for each lesson in a module, time is saved on preparation. As the use of modules has become accepted as part of normal practice, module boxes have been compiled which contain all of the resources used during the teaching of that module. This has assisted with resource banking and has also supported forward planning and budgeting for replacement of consumables in school.

Many of the modules produced also contain prepared worksheets, sometimes aimed at several levels of need, which can then be photocopied for use at an appropriate time. For example, a worksheet which demands some reading ability may be produced for others who use symbols or pictures (see chapter 7). Similarly, sheets containing larger print and less visual detail can be produced for pupils with visual difficulties. By ensuring that worksheets in several formats and accounting for different needs are available in the module, teachers are both assisted by the timesaving factor, and provided with ideas and reminders associated with the diversity of needs. This again has proved its value as a useful timesaver for staff.

Avoidance of unwanted repetition

How often have teachers walked into a staffroom and described in detail a highly successful lesson, only to be told by a colleague, 'I did that with those pupils three years ago' ? Repetition can, of course, play an important role in reinforcing learning for all pupils. We all know, however, that there are some activities which are repeated many times, possibly because they are activities with which both pupils and teachers feel safe. The National Curriculum has, in many instances, assisted staff to consider the breadth of curriculum on offer. The requirements of the National Curriculum mean that we can no longer avoid those more problematic areas of science such as 'forces' for example, and has also encouraged staff to examine areas such as geography and history which were not traditionally well taught in many schools for pupils with learning difficulties (Sebba and Clarke, 1991; 1993).

Curriculum modules related directly to school curriculum policy documents, (as seen in figure 5.2) enable teachers to avoid unwanted repetition. Staff can look back through completed modules and see the content of what has been taught to pupils in the past. The modules also enable staff to build upon the content of previously delivered modules and to select lessons which, through repetition using a different approach, materials, or focus, can build upon existing skills and reinforce processes.

Cross-curricular coverage

The National Curriculum has encouraged some schools to move towards subject focused teaching. This has proved particularly difficult in small schools with limited numbers of staff, and possibly insufficient subject expertise. Some of the curriculum modules developed at Wren Spinney have a definite curriculum focus, as in the example given in figure 5.1. The use of the programmes of study in planning has enabled staff to be clear about which aspects of a curriculum subject are being covered through the module. This assists in planning further work by also highlighting those programmes of study which have not received adequate coverage.

Staff are aware that even when focusing on a specific subject through the use of a module, many opportunities exist to cover programmes of study from other curriculum areas. Equally important is the recognition that further opportunities exist to address important curriculum content which is not related to the National Curriculum core and other foundation subjects. Indeed for many pupils, these areas may be of equal or even greater importance.

Through cross-curricular referencing staff are encouraged not only to examine the skills and knowledge content related to a specific subject area, but also to be clear about opportunities to address the programmes of study from other curriculum areas. Similarly, the modules encourage staff to examine the important processes involved, such as peer interaction, co-operative learning and problem solving by indicating where opportunities exist to foster these.

Differentiation

Modules are written with specific groups of pupils in mind. It is therefore possible to include aspects of differentiation to ensure that individual needs are met. For example, ideas may be included which indicate means of providing physical access through use of technology (see chapter 8) or ensuring correct positioning in specialist equipment such as a prone board or standing frame. Staff can match activities to individual needs, and can equally ensure that group work is encouraged by structuring the activities to take advantage of techniques such as 'jigsawing' (Rose, 1991; Sebba, Byers and Rose, 1993).

As different teachers use the modules with groups of pupils over the years, they add their own notes on providing access or changes to materials which indicate strategies deployed or specific techniques or equipment used which assisted lesson delivery. This serves as a bank of advice which can assist teachers using the module for the first time.

Recording and evaluation

Suggestions for recording activities, including achievement sheets which can be used with photographs, are contained within the modules. In some instances these have included concept keyboard overlays using 'Prompt/Writer' for recording (see chapter 11). This again saves time both in terms of preparation and management of recording systems. Equally important is the opportunity which well produced modules provide for staff to discuss intended lessons with parents, or to report on pupil successes during an annual review. The modules are written in a way which makes them fully accessible to parents, and to other professionals who may be involved either directly, or indirectly, in providing some input during the teaching of a module.

Staff and pupil evaluation sheets built into modules suggest changes for teaching the lessons at a later date as well as providing pupil and staff reactions. These have been kept deliberately brief, with the intention that they should be completed during or immediately after a lesson. The pupil evaluation sheets have been designed to allow enough flexibility for pupils either to complete them alone, or to provide comments for teachers, or to use symbols to indicate the parts of a lesson which they liked, or found difficult (see figure 5.3). Experiments have been conducted which make use of a concept keyboard to provide pupils with opportunities for self evaluation and recording (see chapter 11).

Pupils' involvement in the evaluation of their own work should play an important part in the setting of personal objectives. When used alongside teacher assessment, it can provide useful insights into pupils' interpretations of their own performances. As pupils learn to evaluate their work, they are encouraged to discuss their approach to learning and to negotiate a way forward in building upon their strengths and addressing weaknesses. This also provides an opportunity for staff to clarify their own intentions and to consider their teaching styles in

```
┌─────────────────────────────────────────────────────────┐
│  ╭──────────────────────────────────────────────────╮   │
│  │ Pupil Name  Susan            Lesson No. 7         │   │
│  ╰──────────────────────────────────────────────────╯   │
```

Pupil Name Susan   Lesson No. 7

Did you enjoy the lesson ?
Yes

Which part of the lesson did you like best ?

Making a picture for the room.

Were there parts of the lesson you didn't enjoy ?

No

What was the lesson about ?

Maps. Pictures of things on maps.

Which parts of the lesson were you good at ?

Making a picture. Cutting.

Were there any parts that you were not good at ?

No

Who did you like working with ?
David

Teacher comments.

Comments dictated by Susan to Mary (classroom
assistant)

Figure 5.3: Pupil evaluation sheet

relation to the perceived needs of specific pupils. When pupil self evaluation is used with a number of pupils, it can prove helpful to staff who are concerned to develop effective group work by providing specific indicators regarding individual skills and needs and ensuring compatibility with peers.

Pupil self esteem can be enhanced through self assessment, as they recognise that they are good at some things and that they have progressed as a result of their own endeavours. Furthermore, pupils realise that this progress has been recognised by staff who have, through the evaluation process, an ideal opportunity to offer praise and encouragement. Similarly, an increasing understanding of why there is a need to spend more time on a particular area of weakness can be gained by pupils through the process of self assessment, thus creating a natural opportunity for pupil involvement in setting their own goals.

Such pupil involvement in self assessment, with its aim of ensuring that pupils are clear about their learning objectives and recognise the progress which they are making, makes for more effective learning (see chapter 9) and provides staff with considerable assistance in planning. The whole process of self evaluation is, in itself, a useful area of learning for all pupils, in addition to providing a necessary analysis of specific objectives set for lessons.

Moderation and certification

The school has been able to work closely with NIAS (Northamptonshire Inspectorate and Advisory Service) in order to ensure that the work conducted through curriculum modules is both moderated and certificated. Pupils completing a module have the opportunity to gain a certificate which provides a record of both the experience which they have had through the module, and also the skills and areas of knowledge which have been gained (see figure 5.4). By recording experiences all pupils are eligible for certification, including those with profound and multiple learning difficulties whose achievements may otherwise not be recognised. Skills and knowledge are recorded on a graduated scale enabling pupils to record their achievements whether these are made independently, with some help, or with a lot of help. The certificates are signed by the head teacher, and by the chairman of governors. The inspectorate and advisory services have played an important role through moderation of the modules. This usually involves a member of the service visiting school to observe lessons and talk to staff and pupils about the work involved in the module. At the completion of the module they return to examine work completed, to view displays, talk again with staff and pupils, and assure themselves of the accuracy of assessments made. Certificates are signed by the inspector. These are then presented to the pupils, a copy being retained for the individual Record of Achievement file.

Parents express great satisfaction in receiving certificates which record the experiences and achievements of their sons and daughters.

They particularly value the fact that these have received what is seen as an official assent from an authority outside of the school.

Later developments

Since the introduction of curriculum modules to the school many new developments have taken place. Possibly the most significant of these is a move towards a less teacher directed approach. An examination of the earlier modules reveals that the activities listed give very specific direction in terms of what is to be taught and the materials to be used. Later modules have begun to provide pupils with a greater element of choice and decision making. In some instances this has begun with simple choices over the use of materials and the sequence of activities to be undertaken in a lesson. The introduction of action planning with pupils in the senior groups has expanded upon this with pupils now having more opportunities to define some of the lesson content, and to have a greater say about who they want to work with and how they wish to work. Within the school leavers' course a further element of choice has been introduced with students making decisions about which modules to take during a given period of time.

As staff have become more experienced and skilled in the processes of differentiation and the management of group work, it has become much easier to plan modules which take account of a wider range of individual needs. This, in turn, assists staff to provide an environment which is best suited to the pupils for whom the module is aimed.

Not all of the school curriculum can be delivered through a modular approach. There is still a place for spontaneity and individuality within the timetable of the school, and it would be detrimental to lose this. Modules have, however, encouraged greater awareness of the needs of individual pupils in relation to the overall curriculum. They have promoted a greater breadth and balance of curriculum coverage whilst ensuring that the content is relevant to the pupils for whom they are intended. Equally important is the fact that the school is building a bank of resources which relates directly to the work of staff and is focused specifically upon the school's pupils. The finished modules ensure that good practice in school is no longer lost, and that teachers have well produced examples of their work in which they can take a great pride.

Note: *Prompt/Writer* software is produced by the Special Needs Software Centre, National Council for Educational Technology.

62

Example of Module Certificate

LEARNING ABOUT MAPS

I Can.....
Find places on a map

Identify the countries of the British Isles on a map.

Recognise five map symbols

Use a simple grid reference

Follow simple directions

Cooperate with friends to make a map

Follow a trail around school

Find five rooms on a map of the school

A: Without help.   B: With some help
·C: With a lot of help

This LEARNING ABOUT MAPS MODULE has been moderated by:

Inspector
Northants Inspectorate and
Advisory Service

Side 2: Record of Achievement

WREN SPINNEY SCHOOL

This is to certify that

Completed the module

LEARNING ABOUT MAPS

During the Summer Term 1993

Head Teacher   Chair of Governors

Side 1: Record of Experience

Figure 5.4: Example of module certificate

Chapter Six

A Multidisciplinary Approach to the Whole Curriculum

Caroline Coles

The author is grateful for the support of the Spastics Society and of all the staff at Meldreth Manor School.

Introduction

In this chapter, the author explains how a multidisciplinary approach increases the relevance of the curriculum for pupils with learning difficulties. Team work amongst staff and a commitment to involving parents and the pupil is an effective way of ensuring that the pupils' learning opportunities are maximised.

This chapter is based on the work undertaken at Meldreth Manor School - a school for pupils with physical disabilities and severe and profound and multiple learning difficulties.

Why a multidisciplinary approach?

Access to the National Curriculum alone does not meet all the needs of pupils with learning difficulties. Time is at a premium and there are many calls upon it which are equally as important in a school for pupils with learning difficulties, for instance, physiotherapy, personal welfare, positioning, eating skills, and so on. It may be, in some schools, that each of these important areas is the domain of a different member of staff. Obviously the danger of this for a pupil with severe or profound and multiple learning difficulties is that each of these areas may become fragmented or isolated experiences with no functional meaning for the pupil. A pupil regularly withdrawn from the classroom for therapy, or individual skills sessions, is in danger of learning in isolation. This may lead to them finding difficulties in applying or generalising these skills which could be very counter-productive to their motivation. With-drawal from the classroom by the visiting therapist or specialised teacher perpetuates the segmentation of roles amongst staff. A mystique may develop about the therapist or support teacher's skills and any pupil requiring such support may be viewed as having something separate or supplementary to what is happening in the classroom. Learning opportunities that are delivered in an interdisciplinary context can be more motivating and relevant to the pupil's needs. Therefore collaboration in the planning, teaching and evaluation of the curriculum, will ensure a more consistent approach to the pupils (see chapter 10).

An effective multidisciplinary approach

Effective multidisciplinary working depends on the following staff approach:

- joint planning of learning activities so that there is an agreement on the pupils' goals;
- shared implementation, monitoring and evaluation of pupils' progress;
- effective on-going staff development and joint training systems;
- discussion and agreement about roles and responsibilities.

The team - joint planning

A multidisciplinary team approach in school has to be part of the school's culture. The head teacher and whole staff need to support the principle of teamwork. Mutual sharing, joint working and respecting the skills of others need to be valued and honoured by the school.

Traditional hierarchical school structures can lie uneasy with this approach. A multidisciplinary team approach empowers staff, parents and the pupil. The pupil, parents and all staff (teachers, support staff, therapists) can be directly involved in planning the pupil's learning programme. It is the working practices of the team which will allow more breadth and relevance to the pupil's curriculum. Parents and therapists are an integral part of the pupil's learning experience and it is their full involvement that can support the appropriate delivery of the curriculum. See figure 6.1.

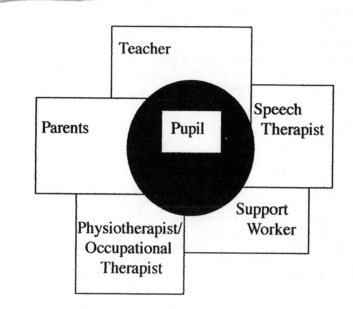

Figure 6.1: The multidisciplinary team

The role of parents

It is vital that the team includes the parents and pupils in programme planning. The involvement of parents allows an 'extended educational day' for the pupil. With parents' knowledge of their child, the most effective way of achieving pupils' learning targets can be formulated. A pupil's dressing programme may also be an opportunity to carry out a physical goal of reaching and stretching. In a day special school a weekly swimming lesson may be the only opportunity to implement this programme in a relevant and motivating context. The regular home routine of dressing and undressing are vital parts of the pupil's learning programme and parents' contributions to the goal setting process are therefore of great importance.

66

NAME: Pamela Johnson DATE: Spring '93 UNIT: Middle	SCHEME OF WORK/MODULE: Growth (People)	CURRICULAR SUBJECT: English/Exp. Lang. KEY STAGE: 3

PoS Speaking and listening
SCHEME OF WORK/MODULE

- Introduce 'feelings' and 'actions' vocabulary
- Giving instructions to peers.
- Miming emotions and actions for others to guess
- Short sketches - act out situations and describe feelings.
- Listen to story 'The Tiger who came to tea'.
- Discuss emotions, items for tiger to eat and think of ending for story.
- Act out story, using files, talkers, etc.
- Video the play and show to pupils for their comments.

INDIVIDUAL OBJECTIVES	SKILL AREAS
1. Pamela will consolidate 'people' and 'feelings' vocabulary using her Introtalker and her Rebus file.	Communication
2. Pamela will integrate her use of the Rebus file and also Introtalker.	Communication/choice and decision making
3. Pamela will develop her creative use of language.	
4. Pamela will orientate herself in a mid line position prior to accessing her communication aid.	Physical

Figure 6.2: A scheme of work for English

The pupil

A pupil's individual curriculum must incorporate the pupil's own preferences and attitudes. The effectiveness of any goal setting for a pupil depends on that pupil's motivation. Pupils with profound and multiple learning difficulties can, and should be, involved in planning their own learning experiences. Some pupils may be able to communicate their needs to make choices by vocalising, facial expression or bodily movement. Some pupils may use photos, pictures or rebus symbols to indicate preferences or perceptions of activities (see chapter 7). Staff and parental knowledge of each pupil's interests, skills and previous experiences will also aid the preparation of relevant and motivating opportunities for the pupil.

INDIVIDUAL RESPONSES

DATE	COMMENT
13.3.93	Thoroughly enjoyed session. Identified people accurately and coped well with new vocabulary.
20.3.93	Once again very motivated. Watched other students with interest and used own board to describe how others may be feeling. Very expressive – enjoyed pretending to be angry! Pamela's sketch – "falling over in mud". She said she was 'dirty' and 'angry' and when asked what she must do she said 'wash'.

INDIVIDUAL RESPONSES

DATE	COMMENT
17.3.93	Story : good grasp of story. Used file to describe feelings of characters and suggest what the tiger might eat. Appropriate use of Introtalker, e.g. greetings 'I'm hungry'. Creative use of Introtalker when did not have vocabulary for cafe. "Let's go outside", "I need my money".
24.3.93	Remembered story well. Chose to be 'Mother' in play. Good use of Introtalker and file as last session.
31.3.93	Enjoyed by all (video). Needed initial prompting to orientate in midline position. Pamela only required minimal prompting by end of sessions to orientate and maintain her midline by using prompt "Think still Pam".

Figure 6.2: A scheme of work for English *continued*

The process of collaborative working

Since full time therapy provision in a school is the exception rather than the rule, it is essential that speech therapists, occupational therapists and physiotherapists see how their own aims for pupils can be incorporated into the teaching or home situation. Many of the exercises planned by therapists can be put into motivating and relevant contexts and do not necessarily warrant withdrawal from the classroom.

At Meldreth Manor School, initial six-monthly or annual reviews, attended by all members of the educational team, give a good opportunity to focus on the pupil's aims in a more 'holistic' way. Once the goals and priorities for the pupil have been agreed and the context for the delivery have been outlined, it is important that staff have an opportunity to work collaboratively together. Collaboration between staff does not occur just by two people working closely together. Effective collaboration is based on the principle that each individual has a valuable and worthwhile contribution to make to the process and that people become resources to each other. In the example, (figure 6.2), the scheme of work for an English lesson was planned for the term jointly by the teacher, speech therapist, physiotherapist and support worker.

Figure 6.3 shows a lesson plan, taken from this scheme of work, which could be delivered by the teacher with the support worker. On occasions the speech therapist or physiotherapist who helped plan this scheme of work could lead the session, giving the teacher an opportunity to take the role of monitoring or recording the pupils' responses. Equally, a therapist could sometimes take this role in the session.

The timetable for such involvement and agreement on staff roles and responsibilities will obviously need to be planned in advance.

Information taken from the record of such sessions, in addition to team meetings, will enable more long term planning to take place. All areas of learning are evaluated and discussed as part of the process of forward planning. Other summative records may include a regular report to parents or Records of Achievement (see chapter 11). A pupil's individual timetable and the balance of time given to each area will obviously change with this process throughout the year, as well as from year to year.

The multi-disciplinary process is shown in figure 6.4.

Staff development

Staff development will never have an impact on practice if it is just grafted on to a school in the form of discrete or unconnected areas. A commitment to multidisciplinary working requires a great deal of flexibility on the part of staff and an openness for evolving and developing their own practice. Effective joint training can transform the delivery of a pupil's curriculum from the situation shown in figure 6.5 to a multidisciplinary approach as shown in figure 6.6.

Inservice training days are an opportunity for staff to share their skills to ensure that every staff member has a baseline knowledge in each others areas of expertise, for instance see figure 6.7.

As mentioned previously, fulltime therapy provision in a school is the exception rather than the rule. Because of this, the possibility of direct contact with the pupil may be rather limited. The therapist visiting a school on a weekly or twice-weekly basis cannot provide effective

ACTIVITY PLAN : Feelings and Action Words	Spring Term 1993	
ACTION PLAN	RESOURCES/EQUIPMENT	STAFF
1. Everyone find new people pages in file. Identify people in the room, e.g. "teacher," "SSW", "boy", "girl", "man", "lady".	Students Rebus files and emotions Rebus sheet. White board/pens	A.M. Coe (Teacher) W. Newton (Speech Therapist) J. Shevan (Support worker) T. Leech (Support worker) M. Turner (Physiotherapist)
2. Introduce new Rebus sheet of feelings and actions. Look at section 1 - feelings. Identify different words by asking around the group. (e.g. "How are you feeling?")	Rebus sheet - 4xA4 + 1xA3.	
3. One student can now choose someone in the room to be "on", using people page to identify them. Student tells that person how to feel and they role play accordingly. Repeat for all the feelings shown.	Rebus file.	
4. Introduce section 2 of sheet - actions. Teacher mimes various actions - guessing game to find these on sheets. Repeat as in 3 (above) only this time the student chooses action to be done and manner in which it is to be done, e.g. "jump"		
		Compiled by:- A.M. Coe

Figure 6.3: Activity plan

The Multidisciplinary Process

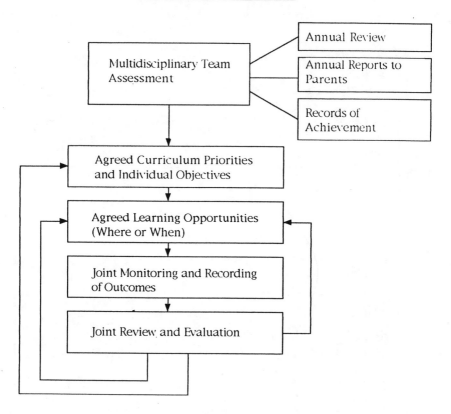

Figure 6.4: The multidisciplinary process

therapy input single-handed; responsibility needs to devolve. Bender (1976) calls this the 'Consultant and Skills Transmitter'. With this model the therapist seeks to increase the impact of his/her skills through their transmission by other workers. This is not to suggest that the therapist abandons all direct work with individual pupils or groups, but that part of his/her time is spent as a trainer of others.

In a day special school this can be done by assigning a classroom assistant for one or two terms to work alongside the therapist when they are in school. Much of the training can be 'hands-on' with informal discussion. A rolling programme in which, over a period of time, all classroom assistants and support staff are assigned to work alongside therapists or visiting specialist teachers, will enable a regular and consistent approach to routine therapy to take place. It will also allow

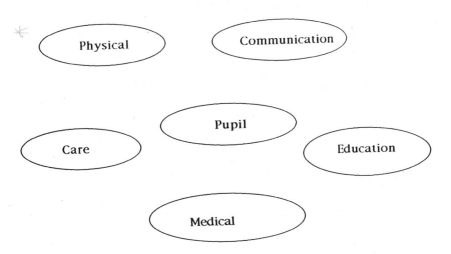

Figure 6.5: Before effective joint training

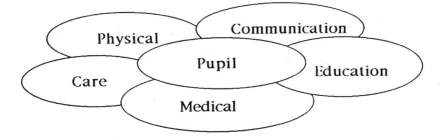

Figure 6.6: After effective joint training

the support staff's knowledge of the pupil and the classroom curriculum to ensure that therapy support forms an integral part of the whole school curriculum.

This process of careful and sensitive role and responsibility rotation lends itself to a sharing of skills, personal and professional growth and enhanced job satisfaction.

The school, and more importantly the pupils, benefit from staff having changed perspectives and a broad outlook to delivering the school curriculum.

SPECIFIC TRAINING WITHIN THE DISCIPLINES

Figure 6.7: Sharing expertise

Conclusion

The change of practice and different way of working at Meldreth Manor School brought a consistency and continuity of approach for pupils seven days a week, throughout their waking day and ensured a focus on the whole child's development. The process of change has involved more than three hundred members of staff who, initially during the period of restructuring, coped with the added stress that a change of role and responsibility brought. However, one notable positive outcome was that all staff became valued members of the team and this, in turn, raised the self-esteem of the support staff.

Finally, an important part of the process in adopting new working practices is that the staff must be involved in the design, implementation and the evaluation of the change. An ethos of collaboration is achieved only by the committed efforts of each individual staff member.

Chapter Seven

Planning for Communication

Ann Fergusson

With acknowledgements to the staff and pupils of Windmill School, Cambridge, all of whom have contributed to the development of ideas presented in this chapter.

Introduction

The pace of curriculum development in schools for pupils with severe learning difficulties has accelerated as a direct result of the Education Reform Act of 1988. The introduction of the National Curriculum challenged all schools to review curricular content and teaching approaches; this is certainly the case within schools for pupils with severe learning difficulties and perhaps in particular with regard to those pupils with profound and multiple learning difficulties. The introduction of the National Curriculum meant that, for the first time, all pupils had an entitlement to the same curricular framework. For many pupils with profound and multiple learning difficulties this was a unique development as frequently they had followed a separate curriculum even from their peers in the main body of their own schools.

The whole curriculum as defined by National Curriculum Council (1990a) shares the same starting points as traditional curriculum models in schools for pupils with learning difficulties, by identifying the individual needs of pupils. Where it begins to differ is in the breadth of curriculum it suggests and specifically outlines in the core and other foundation subjects and in its identification of cross-curricular skills, themes and dimensions. Other differences can be identified in terms of approaches or teaching strategies implied, through the emphasis on encouraging active involvement of pupils, for example, through groupwork (NCC, 1992a; Rose, 1991; Sebba, Byers and Rose, 1993).

This chapter is concerned with the subject area and the processes of communication. Traditionally many special schools would have located this area within categories such as 'Receptive and Expressive Language' or 'Language and Communication'. Here communication is acknowledged to include such traditional definitions, but has its scope widened to include those cross-curricular skills of communication and the English curriculum detailed by National Curriculum Council (DES, 1989b; NCC, 1990a). By redefining this focus, it is possible to draw upon wider aspects of communication, allowing a view of oracy and literacy, for example, as part of the same continuum of processes as the very earliest communicative responses. Similarly it becomes appropriate to draw upon the suggested contexts and strategies outlined in the English programmes of study (for example, speaking and listening in groups of various sizes and for a variety of purposes). This wider definition encompasses the needs and skills of all pupils, even those at very early stages of learning and development and therefore tries to ensure the appropriate mode of access for each individual. This can lead to the identification of appropriate means of access to other areas via the cross-curricular skills of communication. These issues will be explored in this chapter by looking in particular at the ideas of a continuum of communication and a total communication environment.

A communication continuum

In starting with the premise of a communication curriculum addressing the needs of all pupils, it may be useful to view both the processes and skills involved in communication as part of a learning continuum. In this way it is possible to obtain a clearer view while planning for progression of skills. For example, planning for interaction with both the environment and the people in it; planning to develop various communicative roles and the planning of generalising to different contexts or to a wider audience. This notion may also enable staff to be more creative, or selective, in their differentiation strategies when striving to provide pupils with severe learning difficulties with access to the whole curriculum.

The idea of a 'continuum of (communicative) behaviours' was explored by McLean and Snyder-McLean (1985) when looking at early development. Coupe and Joliffe (1988) also refer to the value of mapping

Piagetian sensori-motor stages to such a continuum. If this continuum were also to be seen as interrelated and multi-layered, it would be possible for the wider aspects of the communication curriculum to be included. For example, one layer/level could record the progression of interactive skills. At one end would be early stages of gaining attention, turn-taking, maintenance of interaction, repairing of an interaction (see Goldbart, 1990) for example. Whilst at the other extreme would be the most sophisticated interpersonal skills many of us strive towards ourselves. A separate, but interrelated, layer/level would offer a progression of literacy skills. At the very early stages of this layer/level the associating of objects with particular events (or 'objects of reference') may be a start to realising that certain 'symbols' convey meaning (Ockelford, 1993). At a much more advanced stage would be reading or writing using traditional orthography. A further development may be the understanding of scripts used in other cultures which bear no resemblance to our own print.

Every pupil would join the continuum at their appropriate levels on each layer. They may therefore be at different points on each layer of the continuum, but because of the interrelationships between each layer or aspect of communication, skills and experience could be transferable and generalised. This assumes that pupils are given opportunities to access each layer.

The idea of this continuum is beneficial when planning to broaden and give access to all areas of the curriculum. It can be particularly useful when planning for active and appropriate involvement of all pupils in group or collaborative work. Some practical suggestions are outlined later in this chapter.

A total communication environment

Ideally for every individual to progress along the continuum of communication, the learning environment must, for example:

- offer frequent and consistent opportunities to communicate;
- create a need or desire to communicate;
- provide access to a means of expression (whether non-vocal or other), with plans for progression for every individual;
- view all means/modes of communication as having equal value;
- be consistently responsive to every communicative attempt.

Some valuable general principles for consideration when planning to create such opportunities are described by Sebba, Byers and Rose (1993) in their chapter on personal and social development.

Effective learning opportunities will be those which:

- are relevant to pupils' day-to-day reality and have a clear meaning and purpose for them;
- take account of pupils' interests, aptitudes, experiences and skills and engage the whole child;
- are interactive, encouraging exploration and problem solving through partnership and dialogue between peers and between pupils and teachers;
- are intrinsically motivating, promoting pupil initiation and facilitating self-assessment through shared performance criteria. (p.90)

These ideas are further expanded in chapter 9 of this volume.

In order to create a learning environment that is effective both in offering opportunities to communicate and in being consistently responsive to all communicative actions, there is great value in adopting the idea of total communication. A useful definition of what is traditionally accepted as total communication is offered by Kopchick and Lloyd (1976, p. 503) who suggest it is:

> utilization of all available language modes for the purpose of achieving communication, such as gestures, postures, facial expressions, tones of voice, formal speech and nonspeech systems and simultaneous communication. (Here 'simultaneous communication' is used to mean manual signing accompanied by speech.)

Using such a definition, along with the general principles already suggested, would imply an environment where communication was accepted as being multi-modal. Not only would all modes of pupil-communication be accepted as being potentially meaningful but all those working in the environment (both adults and pupils where possible) would be aware of this potential, and be consistent and sensitive in responding to these various modes. In addition, models of communication by adults (and encouraged in pupils) would utilize and echo the modes used by the pupils themselves. For example, all adults would need to be consistent in their use of sign language (not to say at least as 'fluent' as the most able pupil-signer!) in their interactions with pupils and other adults alike. This gives the message that signing is valued as a means of communication, and offers a good model for pupils.

Similarly the use of visual modes of communication (such as photographs, pictures, and rebus symbols) must be consistently applied throughout the environment by being readily available and standardised rather than limited to certain areas of the environment or even to certain aspects of the school day or timetable. It is easy to forget that these symbols are not automatically as available as speech or signing and that provision should be made for duplicated resources in the kitchen, on the minibus, on the side of the swimming pool, for example. Similarly, a means of transporting communication boards, books or bags of tangible symbols needs to be considered at the stage of planning and designing these aids.

Implementing a total communication environment requires that accurate assessments are made and frequently updated. Just as importantly, this information must be shared with *all* those involved, including the pupils and their peers. This aspect is often overlooked however obvious it may seem. Failure to address these issues will restrict the opportunities for success from the outset, in addition to perpetuating the adult-dominated audiences in which they can be seen as communicating beings. It can be very reassuring to a pupil for an adult to be quite clear in telling them what is expected of them and how the adult will interpret this. Examples could be 'Would you like a drink Vicky? Will you move your mouth to tell me "yes"?', in the case of a youngster who has some consistency in making this response for things she appears to want or like. Or 'Great Jen, you're using your voice and signing "yes" to ask for another swing.' Both examples are clear in reinforcing and acknowledging the communication attempts and the interpreted intention of the communicative attempts (by the adults). Similarly this clarification may heighten the awareness of the pupils' peers and offer a model for them to adopt in order to interact with these pupils in a meaningful way.

The model of total communication used by Kopchick and Lloyd (1976) offered a 'communication program that is available throughout the client's total environment'. Their research was based in a residential setting. Most schools, however, are not in a position to be able to deliver a 24 hour curriculum consistently (see chapter 6), but staff can strive to ensure the consistency of opportunities and responsiveness offered by all those involved with pupils both in and out of school. This obviously has huge implications for ongoing training of staff, parents and carers, visiting professionals and others involved. Similarly, additional demands are made on resources and aids for communication (to allow duplicate sets of materials to go home for example) many of which are time-consuming 'school-produced' items .

The use of augmentative communication

Signing and the use of symbols, in whatever form, may prove of value for all pupils with learning difficulties. From one perspective such augmentative systems may be beneficial to a pupil's development directly, for example when it may be used as an alternative form of communication to speech or, at a later stage, when its use is as a confidence-booster with things unfamiliar. Another aspect of the value of such systems is revealed when they are used as a 'common medium' to enable and promote interaction in particular between pupils themselves, but also with those outside of the home or classroom.

It is important, particularly in the early stages, to be aware of the need to select personal sign and symbol vocabularies for each pupil to match her individual needs, interests, preferences, range of activities and potential 'listeners'. Referents for people or names are very important for the majority of pupils and yet signs or symbols (such as finger spelling initial letters of names or descriptor signs such as 'glasses') are often omitted until later stages. The idea of individual vocabularies may not fit comfortably with the suggested pre-set stages outlined by some systems. However it is very hard to justify feeling unable to introduce a much-needed sign because the pupil has not yet completed all the earlier set-stages of signs.

When considering the most appropriate form of augmentative communication for each pupil, staff need to be clear about her particular learning needs and her current interests and preferences for interaction. Plans for potential progression need to be identified, where possible, from the outset. It is all too easy to begin introducing one specific mode of communication, the pupil achieving great strides, only to come up against a brick wall because, given this pupil's particular learning needs, this mode is quite restricting for a whole range of reasons. For example, pupils with a visual loss may require tangible objects of reference or pictorial symbols with a sensory dimension (such as touch or smell). However, when planning for progression it may be desirable also to introduce signing. The symbols may help to interpret or reinforce the meaning of the signs, which may initially be performed passively with adult (or peer) assistance. In the longer term, signing may provide not only constant access to a means of responding to communication, but also the means of initiating interaction or making requests of someone else. On the other hand, for someone with restricted mobility (for example due to a visual impairment) symbols are not always to hand or easy to find. Again, by way of a contrast, a pupil may have all the necessary skills to understand and produce an extensive sign repertoire, but choose not to use them because she finds face-to-face interaction difficult. The availability of a different visual or tangible mode such as rebus symbols or objects of reference, may offer this pupil the detachedness or objectivity she needs at this time in order to communicate effectively with anyone.

By ensuring the learning environment is multi-modal, utilising total communication principles, staff become more able to meet the individual needs and learning styles of their pupils. The idea of the continuum allows staff to plan for progression either by using one specific mode or system or by combining systems (as illustrated in the earlier example) for the purpose of reinforcing meaning or potentially offering the necessary additional support in unfamiliar situations (a new 'listener', for example).

Each context for learning must provide the necessary clues for pupils to understand their environment and to make activities meaningful. These clues are going to differ for individuals depending upon their location on the communication continuum. Ouvry (1991) outlines such clues for those who are at very early stages of learning. They 'should be carefully planned to intensify the features which identify each situation so that pupils can recognise the activity . . . anticipate their role . . . and enable them to be active participants' (p.46). These clues are of great importance for youngsters who are at a pre-intentional stage of communication (see Coupe and Goldbart, 1988, for further details). It is the consistency of using such clues that may enable them to move into a more active, anticipatory stage. For example the consistent use of body-signing or objects of reference to mark specific actions or activities may lead to the pupil anticipating what is going to happen next and allow her to join in, rather than being completely passive. For instance the body-signing of 'up' by lifting arms upwards to alert a pupil that they are about to be moved into a sitting position may eventually lead to the pupil lifting her head whilst being moved to sitting. The use of passive signing of 'dinner' accompanied with holding a spoon may lead to a pupil mouthing in anticipation of food.

The use of augmentative communication can facilitate and support communication at all levels with consistent use. In terms of planning for progression such systems can be usefully viewed on a continuum. For example, the use of symbols may start with physical symbols such as those mentioned previously - body signing, tangible objects, smells or sounds that act as referents to particular actions or events. Where appropriate the use of visual modes can be introduced to convey meaning in the form of sign language or pictorial symbols (photos, drawings, rebuses) for example, leading finally to the written word. Graphical symbols such as rebuses may be used in the longer term to support the written word, as an aid to reading.

The idea of a continuum offers clear guidance in defining differentiation and progression. It allows the planned introduction of the 'next stages' whilst practising current and newly emerged skills. For example, using tangible objects of reference or photographs concurrently with rebus symbols or similarly rebus symbols with the written word may offer a necessary perceptual bridge between the context and the symbol or word (Carpenter, 1991a). Additionally, by offering the support of more than one stage of symbols at one time, access is possible to a much wider audience (pupils and adults) and therefore creates more opportunities for pupils to interact with each other.

If augmentative modes of communication are adopted to reinforce the links between all aspects of communication (including speaking and listening, reading and writing), there are many implications for the school environment. That 'information must be accessible or convey meaning to all pupils' may provide a guiding principle. An example of such differentiation can be demonstrated through the daily class timetable. It may comprise a sequenced box of objects of reference for one pupil, photographs for another and rebus symbols accompanied by words for the remainder.

Developing the learning environment

Implications for a whole school philosophy on consistency of approach, recognition of communicative modes and the need for staff training in signing have previously been mentioned as being necessary in developing a total communication environment. To reflect this notion within the communication continuum, there may be other features that need to be offered particularly for those pupils at early stages of the continuum. The practical suggestions which make up the rest of this section are presented in note form for ease of reference.

Establishing anticipation or intention

It may be useful to:

- set up consistent routines for:
    - times of the day, e.g. special 'hello' song
    - particular activities, e.g. refer to armband, towel and chlorine smell before swimming
    - ways of moving and handling pupils, e.g. body signing
    - greetings and goodbyes - make them different;

- identify clues to be used, for example:

  - body-signing or passive signing (also need to identify what is to be signalled and how)
  - same adult works with pupils for specific activity, e.g. lunch-time, swimming
  - smells, sounds, e.g. taped music for assembly, smell of oil for massage
  - parts of equipment to be touched before pupil placed in it, e.g. knobs and velcro on standing frame, vinyl of wedge
  - different areas to denote different activities, e.g. singing on carpet, side-lying board for computer, specific chair for lunch;

- collect objects of reference:

  - for each timetabled activity
  - to mark areas/activities around school, e.g. lightroom, kitchen, ballpool
  - to identify people;

- develop a range of activities to explore cause and effect:

  - switch-use, e.g. toys, music, stories, lights, vibrator, fan
  - resonance board and range of different material, e.g. a collection of musical instruments, a collection of everyday objects, a collection of materials with different properties
  - 'little-room' (Nielsen, 1992) with something to touch and locate all around
  - sensory/light rooms or smaller classroom-sized light/sensory boxes;

- offer choices:

  - at meal/snack times
  - of positions
  - of activities
  - of person(s) to work with;

- provide frequent sessions of interaction games that focus on:

  - pupils' present interests and skills (e.g. vocalising, clapping)
  - activities pupils like and may want repeated ('more')
  - activities/movements/sounds pupils initiate and the adult copies or continues (see Nind and Hewitt, 1988 for more on this approach);

- make regular and accurate assessments (try *Affective Communication Assessment*, Coupe et al, 1985):
  - to identify consistent responses
  - to interpret or attach intention or meaning to responses
  - to identify likes and dislikes, needs, preferences
  - to identify items and activities which may encourage the use of these responses to convey identified interpretation of meanings
  - sharing of this information with all involved.

Use of visual modes

(a) Signing

- introduce sign language
  - 'vocabulary' to meet needs and interests of the pupils (ie. individual needs-led vocabulary and whole school 'core' vocabulary)
- raise standard and level of signing by all adults
  - (including lunchtime staff, visiting professionals, etc.)
- organise signing workshops
  - for parents/carers/siblings
  - for peers in other schools.

(b) Photos

- 'who is here today?'
  - individuals find and stick up their own photo
  - match photos to names
- photographs of specific activities
  - useful to refer to 'what we are doing today' and link easily to symbols or a symbol timetable
  - enable some pupils to make choices about the activities they would like to do or for some youngsters the position they would prefer to be in to take part in the activity (e.g. photos of standing-frame, side-lying boards, etc.)
- to identify people, actions or activities
  - class members, family, people who come into contact with pupils regularly or less frequently

- pupils demonstrating 'actions', e.g. eating, drinking, swimming

- to illustrate the outcome of an activity

    - pupils involved in painting alongside their 'end product' for example

- personal books

    - photos about themselves, their family, favourite toys, pets, etc.
    - use to match to cassettes of family 'voices' or familiar sounds from home

- class books

    - to depict specific events or everyday routines, with pupils themselves taking part
    - highlight the 'sequence' of events when retelling the story of what you did
    - tactile stories (Fuller, 1990) for sensory aspects of stories or make your own using objects of reference, e.g. a book on 'what we do on Tuesdays'

- homemade stories

    - using photos, make up a story '. . . about a girl called Ranji...' and include familiar adults and children

Photo albums often have easy to turn pages. Photographs are often stimulating to encourage visual attention. Such books can be the context for achieving joint attention from adult and the 'reader'. Photographs are a simple way to demonstrate that symbols can convey meaning and that they can be appropriate to a wide audience.

(c) Rebuses and the written word

- identify a core vocabulary to meet needs across school

    - it may be necessary to create some symbols, e.g. to match all timetabled activities like science, lightroom, drama, ballpool (see figure 7.1)

- standardise use

    - especially newly created symbols (throughout school, LEA)
    - always use symbols accompanied by words - the size of one may be enlarged to focus on one system (the other mode supporting it)

lightroom   ballpool

Figure 7 1: Lightroom and ballpool symbols created in school

    – standardise methods of altering symbols to convey variations in meaning, for example, possessions or people's names using initials attached in a circle to symbols; an activity rather than a room for the activity, e.g. cooking and kitchen are made different by adding a square around cooking to convey that it is the 'room for cooking'

- endeavour to support any information around the school with symbols (and photos), e.g. displays, labels, directions, door plates, menu board, worksheets, records

- develop a bank of symbol (and word) boards
  - for timetabled activities
  - for each topic
  - for particular events, e.g. school outings
  - for snack or mealtimes
  - for feelings
  - for people
  - as a focus for discussion and recall of events and activities, e.g. items needed to go swimming, sequence of actions to make a sandwich (see figure 7.2)

- resource banks of
  - symbol (and word) cards (see figure 7.3)
    ... for prediction and planning by pupils
    ... to put into card wallets as a daily 'diary' to take home
    ... for use in 'breakthrough to literacy' activities
  - worksheets and record sheets using symbols
  - sticky labels with symbols (and words)
    ... for pupil recording or home-school diary
    ... also for activities mentioned above (photocopiable labels are a useful method for 'mass production')
  - build up a range of computer software using symbols and words (Beste and Detheridge, 1990, Gummett and Martin, 1992 and see chapter 11)
    ... in addition overlays using symbols (also use of tangible symbols)
    ... switches labelled with symbols
- develop library of books with text supported by symbols
  - using photo albums of people, events, activities in school
  - to support story tapes
  - using 'real books', comics, magazines
  - school newsletter
  - using recipes
  - offer pupil 'readers' to move around school to read photo/symbol/word books to other pupils
- link with other schools (see figure 7.4)
  - to exchange and copy school-produced materials, books and games
  - to standardise symbol use between schools.

A wide range of practical examples are documented on the use of symbols (Carpenter, 1991b; Devereux and van Oosterum, 1984; staff of Blythe School, 1986; van Oosterum, 1991). Work by Ackerman and Mount (1991) offers extensive suggestions and activities for developing a 'literate environment' in schools for pupils with severe learning difficulties, many of which would be greatly enhanced by the use of symbols.

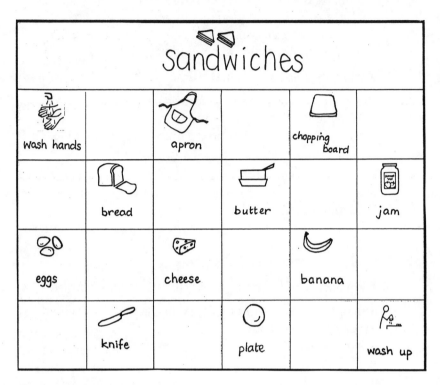

Figure 7.2: Symbol board

Communicative roles

Traditional behavioural approaches, where outcomes are predetermined and teaching contexts are structured, seem to present a mismatch with the spontaneity of communication. This approach has an emphasis on one-to-one teaching programmes and undervalues group work and collaborative learning (Aherne et al, 1990a; McConkey, 1987; Sebba, Byers and Rose, 1993). It is little wonder, for these reasons, that pupils find difficulty in developing the necessary skills to interact with their peers if they have been taught in isolation.

An environment offering the support of augmentative systems and with staff who are sensitive and consistent in responding to communicative attempts, will enable all of our pupils to be more actively involved. This is the first part in planning to develop the communicative roles our pupils play.

Figure 7.3: Symbol card wallet 'diary'

Behavioural approaches by nature are adult-directed, creating an imbalance of power between adult and pupil. Similarly the role of the pupils is limited in contributing to the process of communication and more generally, learning. The role that the pupil plays is one of re- sponder rather than initiator. It is perhaps for these reasons that many youngsters 'get stuck' at certain stages of communication. They are only used to responding and therefore will wait for an adult to initiate interaction. Those pupils who perhaps sign 'please' in response to everything will find great difficulty in shifting to a more active role where they are given opportunities to make choices. Similarly there are pupils who perform their full repertoire of signs because they know they are expected to produce one - they're just not sure which! (or why?).

During a review of approaches using more precise methods such as curriculum audit (see chapter 4) staff may become aware of other imbalances. For example an audit of the delivery of English may highlight the imbalance of proportions of time pupils spend as 'listeners' rather than (in the broadest sense) 'speakers'. Again this situation is reinforcing the pupil role of responder in the communica- tion process. In some cases this may reflect early stages of communica- tion. However, planning needs to ensure that pupils not only have opportunities but the necessary skills to fulfill both roles. There are implications also for the roles of staff.

Staff need to plan to develop the pupils' range of communicative roles. McConkey (1987) and Aherne et al (1990a) describe this ap- proach as moving from an adult-directed situation to those which are

Weather Report

We think that it will be cold this winter with wind, rain, snow and some sun. We like winter. Snow is good. Rain is bad.

Figure 7.4: Article from a school newsletter - George Hastwell School, 1992

child-initiated. The balance needs redressing by ensuring that purposeful contexts are planned in which communication can be functional and meaningful and in which as Mittler (1988) and Goldbart (1990) suggest, there is a real need to communicate. In addition, staff need to ensure that pupils are given opportunities to learn and practise those skills necessary to play a range of communicative roles including, importantly, those of interacting and working with their peers and in groups. Staff need to acquire skills of responding flexibly to unplanned interactions from pupils whether these be spontaneous requests, un-predicted choices or any other form. Where pupils initiate a lead-role staff must learn to follow!

Note: The availability of certain resources mentioned in this chapter is as follows:

From Pictures to Words, Beste, R. and Detheridge, M. (1990), Widgit Software, 102, Radford Road, Leamington Spa, Warwicks.

The Affective Communication Assessment, Coupe, J., Barton, L., Bar-ber, M., Collins, L., Levy, D. and Murphy, D. (1985), Manchester Education Committee, from SERIS, 11 Anson Road, Manchester M13.

Learning with Rebuses: Read, Think and Do, Devereux, K. and Van Oosterom, J., (1984), National Council for Special Education, Strat-ford upon Avon.

Tactile Stories, Fuller, C. (1990), Resources for Learning, The Consor-tium, London. Tel: 071 736 8877

Special Needs IT newsletter from Northwest SEMERC (Oldham), Fitton Hill CDC, Rosary Road, Oldham OL8 2QE.

Chapter Eight

Information Technology across the Curriculum

David Banes and Caroline Coles

The authors wish to acknowledge the work of the staff and students at Meldreth Manor School.

Introduction

There remains a cult in education built around small humming machines that sit in classrooms all over the country. Devotees of this cult meet together on a regular basis in secret to discuss the lore of their arcane craft. Terms such as megahertz bus, ram and PC compatible are swopped and bandied and regularly they create new and more complex terms to confuse and disorientate the uninitiated. But their god is an insatiable one and constantly demands more investment and leaves by the wayside those who cannot successfully purchase the latest upgrades. The authors of this chapter are survivors of this insidious cult who despite their experiences remain interested in the area of educational technology and moreover in the ways in which technology can be harnessed to meet the needs of pupils with a range of learning difficulties.

The purpose of this chapter is not to initiate anyone into the cult described above. We opted out of this way of thinking when we realised that we didn't understand a word of what we were saying. We know that a 33Mhz PC is 'faster' than a 25Mhz one. But have no idea why that might make it better, and moreover have no idea what a Mhz is anyway! Therefore we intend to concentrate on the use to which educational technology can be put in the classroom, by staff with a merely basic knowledge of how to put the machine together, but with the skills and imagination which characterise good teaching across the curriculum.

When we speak of information technology we are not only thinking of microcomputers. We mean that range of devices that can be used to store information and through which information can be made available to pupils easily. A computer is one such system, but so are video players, tape recorders, telephones and fax machines. A mains control box and light switches are equally valuable in facilitating understanding in pupils. Whilst many of the examples that we offer will be related to computers we would not like to suggest that these other forms of technology are any less valuable.

Finally, before getting to the core of this chapter, can we offer our golden rule for the use of microtechnology in schools:

> *no matter how tempting, no matter how much money you have spent, no matter how much the IT co-ordinator implores you, never use computers as the only means of teaching a skill that can be better taught using another means.*

Information technology in the National Curriculum

Information technology is an important part of the National Curriculum. It appears in the curriculum documents in two ways. First it forms one of the two profile components which make up the technology programmes of study. 'Information Technology Capability' consists of five strands; these are:

- communicating information
- handling information
- modelling
- measurement and control
- applications and effects.

Later in this chapter we will examine these areas in a little more detail.

The second element of information technology use in the National Curriculum is the way in which it permeates each of the curriculum documents. Information technology is mentioned in most documents as a specific means of teaching a part of the curriculum, as a means of accessing some of the content of the curriculum described. Information technology is also identified as one of the cross-curricular skills running throughout the whole curriculum. In practice, these two forms overlap and inter-relate with one another, re-emphasising the need to consider the role of information technology in the whole curriculum.

In order to consider these issues this chapter is divided into four sections:

- physical access
- progression and continuity in using switches and software
- teaching approaches, learning styles, and information technology
- information technology and the integrated scheme of work.

Physical access to information technology

The form of access that you develop with a pupil may be put to a variety of purposes, such as mobility, communication aid or simple switch software. Therefore the first feature of exploring access is not the switch itself but the interface with the equipment that is being used. These may take the form of a switch box, or perhaps a more complex piece of electronic wizardry. Before choosing a piece of equipment it is important first to examine how any switch could be plugged into it.

It is worthwhile to try to plug a switch in. There are a plethora of switches available. Many staff find it useful to keep a list of the switches that are currently available, with a photograph of each, which will help a member of staff to suggest a switch that is worth trying for an individual. Materials produced by the ACE centre can be of value here. If you think this seems obvious, we visited a school where a £100 joystick stood unused because it arrived at the school with a 5 pin din plug and no-one at the school knew how to plug this into their computers.

In identifying an appropriate switch for a pupil, we suggest that the aim is to find a reliable, repeatable and comfortable access system. With many pupils who have severe learning difficulties this is likely to be through a simple switch, although other possibilities such as a touchscreen or concept keyboard should not be ruled out.

It is important in considering which switch to use that the assessment is carried out in a multidisciplinary way. There will need to be a consistency of positioning or seating and staff working together must ensure that the work that is completed on the computer does not become a fragmented or an isolated experience with no relevance to the other learning opportunities in the school.

To achieve success the following principles should be applied:

Seating

If pupils are having to think about, and work at, positioning themselves, then they are incapable of attending to or thinking and concentrating on the computer program or communication device.

Switch positioning

Pupils using a switch or touchscreen may need the computer keyboard out of sight and reach so that it is not a distraction.

The switch should always be in the same position, fixed with velcro or clamped, so that the pupil is used to the position and can concentrate on looking at the screen rather than finding the switch.

The screen needs to be in the best possible position for the pupil without any light reflecting upon it. The pupil needs to be happy with the access method and some cosmetic work might need to be done on the actual switch to make it acceptable. Equally, visually impaired pupils might need a tactile cue added to the switch so that they can easily locate it.

Reward

If the pupil has any form of sensory impairment it is important to consider if the reward is satisfying to the pupil. Any sound reward may need to be amplified to be successful with a pupil with a hearing impairment, whereas a pupil with a visual impairment may need a bright, moving, visual reward in addition to a tactile switch or switches.

Periods of time

When introducing a new piece of hardware or software, it is essential that the sessions are restricted to short periods initially. The sessions on the computer should be fun and enjoyable and the atmosphere relaxed. A number of short, pleasurable sessions in a day are likely to be more successful than longer sessions at infrequent intervals.

To summarise, to implement all of these principles there needs to be a commitment to microtechnology by all the staff involved with a pupil. The computers and communication devices that we are accessing through these means need to be an integral part of all classroom activities and not simply something that happens on a Wednesday afternoon when a pupil is withdrawn from class.

If the technology is integral to all activities then it becomes essential that information about pupil progress is monitored and recorded.

Recording

A method of recording each pupil's use of the computer is important to avoid endless repetition of the same or of an unsuccessful program. A recording sheet will need to be kept for every student. However, any such recording must be quick, simple, clear and precise. A sheet needs to contain (see figures 8.1 and 8.2):

- the name of the program and where it can be found
- the type of access (touchscreen, lever switch etc.)
- the position of the switch (easily facilitated by the skilful use of stick figures or, for the unartistic, polaroid photographs)
- comments and observations.

Switch progression

One of the major difficulties that schools experience in using microtechnology is ensuring that software and hardware are organised to ensure that pupils progress and that staff have some idea of the next step to take with a pupil. We are familiar with examples of pupils who have worked with the same piece of software day after day and year in, year out whilst at school.

Individually, microtechnology allows a pupil to move from being a spectator (using the computer for sensory stimulation) to being a participant (interacting with their learning environment in ways that affect the outcome) and then on to creator (beginning to extend or alter their environment).

Certain types of computer programs can allow a natural shift along this continuum - from spectator to participant to creator - and thus give the pupil more control over their own lives.

The switch progression we have arrived at (after many revisions) looks very simple. All of the software is grouped into one of five levels, these levels are then further subdivided into stages corresponding to the input device that is being used, (see figure 8.3).

Level 0

As a spectator, the pupil is mainly watching, listening or passively responding. The relationship between them and their learning environment is one where they are regarded mainly as recipients. In this scenario, technology can enhance sensory awareness, providing sensory or auditory stimulation in an exciting and motivating context.

Computer Information

Name		Date

Age

Seating/Positioning

Sensory Needs

Access

Switching Level(s)

Aims

Programs

Figure 8.1: Recording sheet

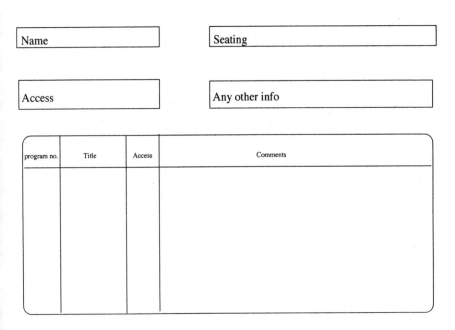

Figure 8.2: Recording sheet

Level 1

As a participant, the pupil is beginning to interact with his or her environment. The pupil can learn that an action, such as touching a switch, can cause a response such as that on the screen. The simplest computer programs involve the pupils in touching a switch or reaching for a computer touchscreen and observing what happens. The action usually produces a response which is bright, colourful, moving and noisy.

Level 2

Programs in the second stage require a pupil to become more discriminating. Each switch press may add another part to a picture and a short animation is usually the final reward.

Level 3

This level requires more skill and accuracy, because the pupil has to respond to the action by switching at a particular time or event. Often the speed/time and size of target and sound can be changed. This stage can be introduced gradually to ensure that the pupil doesn't become

98

Category	Levels			
Spectator	LEVEL 0 Passive no switching			
Participant	LEVEL 1.1 1 Switch single input		LEVEL 1.3 TouchScreen single input	
	LEVEL 2.1 1 Switch Build/Animate	LEVEL 2.2 2 Switch Build/Animate	LEVEL 2.3 TouchScreen Build/Animate	
	LEVEL 3.1 1 Switch Accuracy	LEVEL 3.2 2 Switch Accuracy Joystick 2 directions	LEVEL 3.3 TouchScreen Accuracy	LEVEL 3.4 Joystick 4 directions
Creator	LEVEL 4.1 1 Switch Choice	LEVEL 4.2 2 Switch Choice	LEVEL 4.3 TouchScreen Choice	
	LEVEL 5.1 1 Switch Scanning	LEVEL 5.2 2 Switch Scanning		

Figure 8.3: Software/switch progression

frustrated and that using the computer continues to be motivating and fun.

Levels 4 and 5

These levels are about the pupil making decisions, moving from being a participant to a creator. At this stage the pupil is using the switch or touchscreen to choose the correct answer or scanning to select a word or a picture.

The skill of scanning is an essential one for the operation of a speech machine or of a switch based word/symbol processor. The pupil needs to be accurate at making her selection while using a single switch. Accuracy can be improved by slowing the speed down, but this can result in the program becoming boring for the pupil.

Using two switches, a pupil can establish control over the speed of the scanning, as one switch is pressed to move a highlighter through the options and a second switch then indicates the selection. Pupils may of course have difficulties remembering what each switch does and many teachers have found that putting symbols or even simply colours on the switches may help.

Possibly the greatest cognitive leap that is expected from a pupil in this sequence or progression is between levels 2 and 3. This entails developing from being able simply to press a switch repeatedly and still get a reward and then moving on to having to think about when one presses a switch.

Teaching approaches, learning styles and information technology

In teaching pupils with a range of learning difficulties, staff use a range of contexts for such teaching to take place. In the past one often heard it said that 'real' teaching took place in individual one-to-one sessions with a pupil, implying that group activities were of lesser value, and were often holding or occupational activities.

Happily, this is not a widely held view today. Staff in schools recognise that there are a range of teaching styles available to them, and that different pupils benefit from different styles at different times for different activities. Such a range of styles could include:

- individual learning - learning by rote;
- individual learning - investigations and explorations;
- paired parallel activities;
- co-operative activities involving the sharing of resources;
- collaborative activities leading to a common aim.

Such a selection is of course somewhat random, but serves to illustrate the different contexts in which a pupil might approach a task.

To continue we intend to look at each of these in turn, and consider how information technology can be used to access each of these styles.

Individual learning

This is probably the most common style found in using a computer with pupils with learning difficulties. At the most fundamental level, a one-to-one learning situation is created where one pupil works with one computer, on a repeated task. These could begin with repeated switch presses by a pupil to build a picture on the computer screen, with the

computer animating and clearing the screen every time the pupil finishes a picture. At a more complex level, computers can be used via a
keyboard to complete cloze procedures or sums with immediate feedback and corrections being offered.

In many ways the computer takes the place of the teacher in these
situations. The computer is being used as a complex learning machine,
setting the level and pace at which a pupil is learning according to the
success the pupil is having.

There has been a tendency for such software to be denigrated by
information technology experts over the past few years in favour of
more open styles. But there is still a place for such learning with pupils
who require a lot of practice at a fundamental skill, whether that be
causation or calculation. However as a teacher one would need to ask,
'how else am I teaching this skill, and would this pupil learn this skill
as well or better in a more traditional way?' For instance, the pupil who
is using the computer to complete a list of sums might do better with a
pile of counters and an exercise book. Or might do even better by
practising calculation during a cookery lesson or by adding together
the dinner money for the school secretary on a large calculator. In
summary, the computer should be used to offer complementary ways
of extending a pupil's learning.

Open ended individual learning

As with the closed processes described above, the computer can be used
to facilitate open ended or investigative learning. At an early stage this
could involve a pupil working with two switches which each do different
things. By pressing the switches the pupil learns herself that there are
different effects related to each. Equally a pupil could learn that the
timing of pressing a switch affects the outcome. At a more complex level
a pupil could be working alone with the computer with an adventure
game. This represents the ways in which computers are most used as a
leisure activity and should be valued in that context at least. Using the
keyboard a pupil can map out an imaginary land making a range of
decisions en route.

Framework programs, (those with no specific content), can also be
used. These include word processors and calculators, or a range of art
programs. The computer can be a valuable art tool. Although it lacks
the immediacy and tactile experience of paint, it does have the strength
in that it is easily modifiable, and with pupils with poor self esteem this
facility to correct errors painlessly can be of value.

Paired parallel activities

The first step in creating groupwork with pupils is to think about how pupils are positioned and organised to work. Often it is suggested that pupils with profound learning difficulties work at their best in distraction free environments. There is, however, value in pupils working in ways that encourage them to be aware of the wider environment in which they are working. If a pupil is using a selection of cause and effect software they could be seated in such a way as to be seen by another pupil using the same software, and hence to offer a good role model to the pupil. Such a situation may also help a pupil to understand the relationship between the action and the reaction, the switch and the effect.

With pupils operating at more complex levels similar settings can be constructed. Two pupils using an art package on the computer can see each other's work, as it progresses. They can then use each other as a resource, ask questions of the other as to how an effect is generated, or simply serve as an audience for a piece of work.

The value of paired activities has long been recognised in reading and mathematics. In extending this practice on the computer, we are building upon a firm foundation across the curriculum.

Co-operative activities

The description of paired activities given above can be naturally extended into larger groups and can encourage co-operation between pupils working on the same or different tasks.

At the earliest stages, co-operation can take place when two pupils share in an activity that requires turn taking. Many simple cause and effect programs offer a facility wherein pupils can use two switches to build an image in stages. If each pupil has a different switch then they may discover that they must take it in turns to use the switch to activate the program. With other pupils such co-operation could take the form of sharing a word processor and having to work out for themselves who is going to do some writing, when is it going to be done, and what the other pupil is going to do whilst waiting for her turn. Co-operation can also take the form of pupils asking each other for advice. Spellings, ideas and even how to make a disk start are difficulties that beset the pupil but with which other pupils may be able to assist.

Although in this context pupils may be grouped together for an activity, we cannot really call this groupwork until some form of positive interdependence is being encouraged to develop among the pupils. It is in our final example below that this becomes true.

Collaborative activities

In encouraging pupils to work together in the ways described above we reach a point where dependency upon the others in a group becomes essential if the task is to be completed successfully. This is demonstrated in the example already given where each of two pupils needs the other to press a switch before their own switch becomes active. But we can also look at the adventure game discussed earlier as a context in which groupwork can be developed.

A group of pupils can use a simple adventure game together. Decisions can be made collectively by each pupil having a vote, ('do we go left or right, up or down?'). Equally, different roles can be identified in the group - one pupil makes a map, another works the concept keyboard whilst yet another reads any text on the screen. This allows teachers to differentiate the activity to meet specific individual needs of the pupils within a group, one pupil practising reading, another geography skills. Of course with some support these roles can be changed as the activity develops.

The description given above is of pupils working collaboratively to complete a puzzle or investigation. Staff can also encourage pupils to work collaboratively with the computer in other ways. For instance the production of a class magazine using a computer to typeset the final copy is an option that is easily available to most teachers. In the activity, pairs of pupils can be working together to produce one part of the newspaper. One pair is conducting a survey and using a database to display their results, another pair is collecting photographs to illustrate the news. Different pairs of pupils are writing their stories up, sharing the word processor as they become ready for type setting. Finally, another pair of pupils is taking the stories and cutting and pasting them with the photographs to produce a final product.

In this activity, which could take place over a number of weeks, learning opportunities are created that meet individual needs but which value all the levels of task that pupils are working at. Moreover, we are also using the computer not only as a tool, but also as the central part of the lesson through the desk top publisher. This now leads us to look at using the computer as a focus for integrated schemes of work.

Integrated schemes of work

The integrated scheme of work represents one way of linking the diverse elements of the curriculum into a theme or topic. The computer provides one way of doing this, either by its use as an access tool, as described above in the context of desk top publishing, or by using the content of a program as the basis of a far wider ranging exploration of a theme. To examine this further we can look at a specific example, in this case an adventure program on the BBC computer. Although we will look at the specific content of this program, it is the process of planning that it is intended to illustrate. The program is called 'Microbugs' and is concerned with a character travelling into a magic land to hunt for a lost toy. In doing so, the character must solve a range of mathematical and language puzzles en route.

The process of building a theme around this content starts by brainstorming and extending this computer activity into other areas of the curriculum. This is most often represented in the form of a flow chart, (see figure 8.4). The member of staff here has planned that using the content and inspiration of the program there are natural links into other areas of the curriculum, art, drama, music, maths, language and so on.

Using this as a basis the member of staff can then plan from the appropriate programmes of study around the theme suggested for this piece of software.

In this case the theme suggested by the software was not related to information technology. We could, of course, take a theme directly related to one of the strands of information technology and construct a flowchart around that idea. To take an example we can look at 'communicating information' and brainstorm a related set of ideas, as shown in figure 8.5. The ideas suggested by the flowchart not only offer some further themes to follow up, but naturally suggest activities which will access the programmes of study. The exploration and investigation of this form of technology based around the National Curriculum for technology has obvious overlaps with other National Curriculum areas, notably those of English, science, history and geography. The skills developed in passing on information to the range of audiences suggested in the flow chart can only offer more to the pupils involved in terms of their personal and social development as well.

Summary

In this chapter we have tried to demonstrate some of the potential that information technology has in accessing a broad and balanced curriculum. In doing so we have posed a dilemma for staff in schools. That is: 'How do I incorporate the technology into my good practice without becoming overburdened with the technical skills involved in understanding the technology?' The answer remains to be found by the whole staff

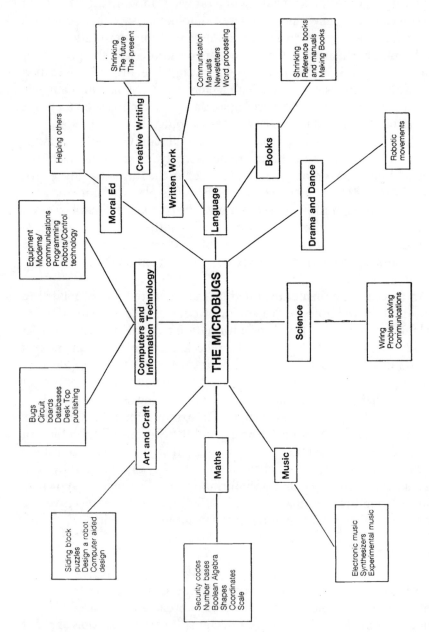

Figure 8.4: 'The Microbugs' flowchart

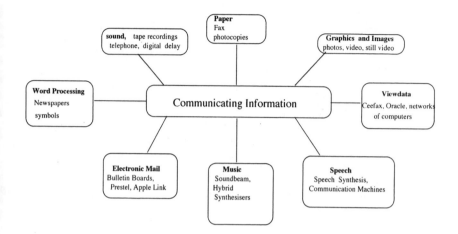

Figure 8.5: Communicating information flowchart

of a school, and the development of a whole school policy, which is manageable and directed by the whole staff rather than the co-ordinator, remains a priority for many schools. In examining the information technology policies of several schools in which we have worked, we note that much of the policy is related to the technical expertise of the co-ordinator. The development of the purchase of hardware and computer peripherals, such as printers, has dominated the thinking behind the policies. Such purchasing plans need to be kept firmly in their place, namely as the means by which a policy is implemented. It is our belief that the policy should reflect the needs of staff and pupils, and not the needs of the equipment!

Note: A range of booklets, including *Switches and Interfaces,* is available from the ACE Centre, c/o Ormerod School, Headington, Oxford.

The MicroBugs: an adventure in information technology for 9 to 14 year olds is produced by Sherston Software, Swan Barton, Sherston, Malmesbury, Wiltshire. SN16 0LH.

107

Chapter Nine

Providing Opportunities for Effective Learning

Richard Byers

With acknowledgements to Tricia Akehurst, Sue Upson and 'Naughty Hilly', with whom many of the following ideas originate, and to Greta Wills, with whom the scheme of work described in this chapter was planned, team taught and recorded.

Introduction

In *Redefining the Whole Curriculum for Pupils with Learning Difficulties,* Sebba, Byers and Rose (1993) proposed that pupils' learning experiences should, in order to be truly effective, encompass both achievement within the basic curriculum (broadly, the core and other foundation subjects of the National Curriculum) and progress in terms of personal and social development. The authors suggested that teaching approaches and learning styles themselves have a significant impact upon pupils' self esteem and self confidence and therefore upon progress towards independence and personal or cultural autonomy. The kinds of learning opportunities which are likely to be effective in terms of pupils' personal and social development were characterised, with acknowledgements to Rogers (1983), Ryder and Campbell (1988) and Friere (1972), as being:

- **purposeful** - relevant to pupils' everyday reality and meaningful in ways which are accessible to them;

- **holistic** - taking account of the whole pupil and engaging a range of pupil interests, experiences, skills and aptitudes;
- **interactive** - promoting dialogue between teacher and learner, between learners and their peers and between learners and the nature of their learning experience;
- **participative** - intrinsically motivating, allowing for pupil self as-sessment through shared target setting and performance criteria.

This chapter will explore these ideas in greater detail and will provide examples of their practical application. Ilustrations will be based upon a single lesson drawn from an integrated scheme of work concerning 'living and growing'. This scheme of work was designed for a group of twelve pupils with a range of severe and profound learning difficulties, some of them with associated physical, behavioural or emotional diffi-culties. These pupils were drawn from three different classes but were all chronologically within Key Stage 3 of the National Curriculum. The intention was to devise curriculum driven, subject focused plans for group activities which could be structured in order to provide a variety of differentiated and effective individual learning opportunities.

Each session was team planned in the context of a whole school topic and was team taught by two teachers and a special support assistant. The particular session described clearly provides access to the pro-grammes of study for a range of National Curriculum subjects - notably technology, geography and science. This chapter will not, however, dwell upon these references as the implications of cross-curricular planning and recording for pupils with learning difficulties have been dealt with in detail elsewhere (Byers, 1992; NCC, 1992a and 1992b).

All the sessions in the 'living and growing' scheme of work aimed to bring together theory, knowledge and understanding with practical activity and pupil recording. The scheme of work included sessions concerning live plants, live animals and objects that are not alive; the basic requirements for sustaining different forms of life; and the char-acteristic movements and responses of living things. Each session in the scheme of work included a deliberately ludicrous, hopefully amusing, introductory section which aimed to engage pupil interest by virtue of its performance element. These bizarre introductions also sought to probe pupil understanding of the issues involved through observation of their responses to the incongruities laid before them. For reasons which will become obvious, staff elected to work with lifelike toy or model animals rather than with real ones.

Many of the ideas in this chapter reflect established and familiar strategies employed by staff in schools for pupils with learning difficulties. These strategies may not, however, be valued as part of a coherent policy with regard to effective practice. This chapter will therefore offer some structure for the instinctive, even idiosyncratic, approaches that many teachers already use and provide examples of some of the ways in which learning theory may apply to pupils with learning difficulties. The bold sub-headings throughout the rest of the chapter may be seen as an *aide memoire* for some of the characteristics of effective learning opportunities while the intervening paragraphs offer practical illustration.

Pupils are involved

All the examples given in this chapter will seek to illustrate the principle that pupils should be involved in their learning rather than being regarded as the passive recipients of wisdom emanating from an external source. Friere (1972), in championing a move away from a view of learners as meek 'receptacles' or 'docile listeners', argues that students should be seen as 'critical co-investigators in dialogue with the teacher.' In practice, such involvement may take a number of different forms for different pupils at different times and at different stages of their individual learning processes. In any one session, some pupils may gain understanding through active participation in a practical task. Others may learn through participation in group discussion or negotiation. Some learners may be ready to participate by listening or by sharing an agreement or understanding with regard to a collective experience. The principle which lies behind involvement of all kinds, however, is that pupils should have access to the meaning and purpose of their activity rather than being subjected to teacher requirements which may, for the pupils, be incomprehensible or incoherent. As Rogers (1983) says, this involves 'the whole person in both the feeling and cognitive aspects being *in* the learning event.' The examples given in this chapter will demonstrate that a variety of different forms of involvement, appropriate to a range of different learning styles, can be accomodated within a single session.

Pupils are cued into the activity

In an ideal situation, all pupils would come to learning activities in a state of readiness, knowing, broadly, what to expect. This is not to say that there should never be surprises or innovations. It is rather to suggest that a situation where pupils drift, or are delivered, from one session to another with very little sense of the structure or plan for their day should be avoided. Pupils in mainstream schools are given access to their timetables in written form. Staff in schools for pupils with learning difficulties bring more imagination and creativity to the task of rendering their timetables accessible to pupils. Spoken language, conventional visual symbols, sounds, scents, sensations and real objects have all been used in order to cue pupils into forthcoming activities (NCC, 1992a and see chapter 7).

The sessions planned for the 'living and growing' scheme of work all took place on a Monday afternoon in the same room. However, because of the mixed aptitude, vertical groupings operating in the school for afternoon sessions, pupils came to this room in different states of preparedness, from a variety of different class bases around the school. Some pupils came from classes where pupil accessible timetables were in use; other pupils were told or knew by association that Monday afternoons meant a class with Richard and Greta; for yet other pupils, arrival at different teaching locations for afternoon sessions appeared to present a constant series of surprises. It was difficult to ensure that pupils were consistently cued into the nature of the Monday afternoon activity before they arrived in the room. Indeed, the room itself was a familiar class base for some of the pupils and a totally unknown space for others.

In order to counteract this disparity and try to transform the room into a particular and memorable environment, a decision was made to make the room characteristically different and consistently recognisable for the Monday afternoon sessions and to provide consistent cues as pupils came in the door. Staff devoted lunchtimes to setting up the room, putting pupils' tables and chairs into a horseshoe pattern around the central teaching and demonstration area. This seating arrangement afforded pupils a guaranteed good view of demonstrations as well as offering good visual and physical access to pupil activities for staff acting as observers and recorders. It also made the subdivision of the class into small working groups easier to manage. With the demonstration table out front covered, hopefully intriguingly, with items of equipment, objects and artifacts, the intention was that the very layout of the room would remind pupils of last week's session and prepare them for a further, related experience.

Attempts were made to start each session in a similar way, with a welcome for each pupil and member of staff and an introduction in which the forthcoming activities were described and some of the items which would be in use shown to the pupils for looking, listening, feeling or tasting.

A decision had been made to begin each session with a burlesque episode designed both as a means of revisiting familiar concepts and experiences and as a way to introduce each week's new subject matter. One week pupils were sent on a crazy trail, looking for items in unlikely places which would emphasise their 'alive' or 'not alive' status. Pupils found rocks growing on trees, an apple sprouting from the clothes line and a shoe which appeared to have taken root in the garden. On other occasions staff offered absurd diets to unsuspecting plants and animals and discovered fish that jumped and rabbits that flew in a farcical introduction exploring modes of movement. The session described in this chapter opened with an illustrated lecture on habitats. Hamming it up outrageously, a bewildered teacher was greeted with howls of derision from a class quick to see this week's joke as a bird was floated in a tank of water; a plant was set to grow in the oven; a fish was settled into a birdcage and a rabbit was shut up safely in a sandwich box.

The whole pupil is engaged

It was clear, from the outset of this session, that pupils were involved. They called out; they laughed; they whooped with a mixture of delight and horror as the anarchy unfolded before them. Some only smiled in recognition of the teacher's folly, but these lower key responses also revealed a measure of understanding and were duly recorded. Some of the comment and hilarity, to be sure, occurred largely in response to the bizarre notion of a teacher 'getting things wrong', but much of it also revealed awareness and understanding. The expression of a realisation that birds do not live in fish bowls was recorded as confirmation of an initial level of knowledge about what birds do need in the way of a habitat in order to survive. Encouraging this sort of awareness was one of the purposes of the lesson.

Pupils' laughter was welcomed for another reason. It was a token of engagement. The theory of effective learning argues that it is not enough simply to challenge pupils academically or in terms of their practical skills. Kolb (1984) describes learning as 'an holistic process of adaptation to the world' and argues:

> To learn is not the special province of a single specialised realm of human functioning such as cognition or perception. It involves the integrated functioning of the total organism - thinking, feeling, perceiving, and behaving. (p. 31)

In this spirit, the session set out to engage pupils as whole persons, capturing their imaginations, tickling their senses of humour, prodding their memories of home or of previous experiences. The laughter and smiles were welcome because they showed that an important aspect of the consciousness of the pupils was focused on the session from the outset. Further, pupils' interjections demonstrated emotional engagement and the exercise of a sense of compassion. Along with the laughter came some sympathetic groans. Clearly some pupils knew that it would be cruel to put the bird in water or to shut the rabbit in a drawer. Pupils not only perceived the jokes because of the incongruity of concepts. They also understood the potential implications of the ludicrous mistakes which were being perpetrated and were moved to feel pity.

This revealed the engagement of yet another important aspect of the pupils' selves. Participants began to volunteer comments about the errors the crazy teacher was making. Some comments were verbal and indicated an awareness that people do not keep rabbits in sandwich boxes or small birds in tanks of water. Some comments were necessarily based on actions as pupils came forward to rescue creatures from the misconceptions of the crazy teacher in order to place them into more appropriate environments. These comments were clearly based on past experience. Where it was possible, pupils' understanding of previous school activities was reinforced during these exchanges. Words for 'leaves' and 'roots' or 'wings' and 'tails' explored during the previous term's scheme of work were revised, for instance, together with ideas from earlier sessions on animal diets. However, much of the awareness pupils brought to the session had its origins outside school. At the planning stage, decisions had been made to deal with creatures familiar from domestic environments. The work on habitats therefore focused upon goldfish, budgerigars, rabbits and geraniums rather than upon anything more exotic.

Pupil comments indicated the wisdom of these decisions as memories of auntie's fish and granny's budgie helped pupils to define their sense of the wrongness of the crazy teacher's actions. In some cases this obviously originated in affection for particular creatures - *our* budgie or *auntie's* goldfish - but for others there appeared to be a more general concept of fair treatment, kind handling or basic rights which took the session far beyond the cataloguing of the necessities for the survival of different forms of life. Another aspect of the whole person as pupil was engaged as memories of home life and of weekends and holidays modified and informed classroom experience.

The significance of promoting the relationship between experience and learning is emphasised by teachers working among adults. John Mulligan (1992) identifies seven internal processes which create useful bridges between experience and learning.

- **Willing:** Mulligan describes willing in terms of choice, intentionality and motivation. It serves to co-ordinate, organise and order the learning process and is 'a function of the whole person' which renders the pupil amenable to teaching and ready to learn.

- **Remembering:** This chapter has already explored some aspects of remembering, the second of Mulligan's internal processors which, he emphasises, operates at a number of different levels. Memories may be sensory, symbolic, conceptual, verbal or physical, expressed through responses described as reflex actions. The experiential facilitator will be competent in encouraging the learner to dip into all these remembering processes in the course of her learning.

- **Reasoning:** Abstact reasoning is often seen as the supposedly objective, rational process whereby experience is clarified in order to permit explanations, interpretations, predictions or even descriptions. As such it is clearly essential to scientific exploration in the National Curriculum. Mulligan insists, however, that one of the important aspects of experiential learning is that conventional constructs and frameworks should be challenged and established beliefs suspended. It could be argued that the burlesque introductions to the sessions in the scheme of work described in this chapter constitute one way of encouraging pupils to re-examine their preconceptions and established models of conduct, even if only at the level of 'teachers always behave sensibly'. As Kolb (1984) argues:

  If the education process begins by bringing out the learner's beliefs and theories, examining and testing them, and then integrating the new, more refined ideas into the person's belief systems, the learning process will be facilitated. (p. 26)

- **Feeling:** Mulligan asserts that emotional fluency is as significant in the learning process as rational clarity. Blocked feelings can impede learning in as profound a way as fractured reasoning. Any attempt to engage the whole pupil will therefore need to bring forth emotional responses.

- **Sensing:** There will be no need to emphasise the significance of first hand sensory experience to staff involved with pupils with learning difficulties. Suffice it to say that Mulligan extolls the virtues of a sensory approach, to art and science for instance, for all learners.

- **Intuiting:** Mulligan describes intuition as complementary to sensing yet also its opposite. Where sensation focuses upon external sources of stimulation, the intuition listens to an internal voice in order to gain access to 'a form of direct knowing.' Intuition will lead the learner to the core of things; to the relationships between ideas; and often towards useful starting points for enquiry or hypothesis. It is difficult to see how intuitive processes could be deliberately developed in pupils, or revised or practised. Mulligan argues that intuition can be 'allowed', however, by encouraging learners at times to be in 'a state of passive-receptive expectant attention.' For those whose preconceptions categorise effective learning as universally active, this constitutes another argument in favour of preparing learning opportunities which will accomodate variety and balance in terms of learning styles.

- **Imagining:** Mulligan stresses the power of the imagination in learning and its fundamental significance to creativity and action. He also asserts that imagination can enable the learner to transcend current reality and to 'try out new roles and behaviours without having to become committed to them' while avoiding the 'high risk of personal exposure to the real life consequences.' The imagination has a role to play in encouraging learners to peer through apparent restrictions and into a world of 'What if?' possibilities. In this sense, learning opportunities which stretch and challenge the imagination will have a useful contribution to make to pupils' personal and social education.

This brief examination of one analysis of the complexity of whole person learning will strike some chords of recognition with ideas that follow in the rest of this chapter and present some serious ideological challenges for staff who are themselves learning about learning with learning difficulties. Next time the idea of whole pupil engagement is bandied loosely about, it may be salutory to recall Mulligan's set of seven internal processors. For the moment it is, perhaps, enough to recall that this chapter is describing the opening burlesque sequence of a session which, hopefully, has engaged pupils' goodwill; called forth some memories; challenged certain existing rational constructs; elicited emotional and sensory responses and provided some imaginative, even whimsical, links between ideas.

Any performance criteria are shared

With the burlesque session quietening down, any comments from pupils, whether verbal, gestural or expressed in action, were noted and validated and used to propel the session towards its next stage - using pupil suggestions as to what might make better habitats for the creatures assembled in the room. Some pupils had already demonstrated that they knew that the fish 'ought' to live in the tank of water. The session now moved towards a focus on why this should be the case. As pupils explored the notion that plants need a place to grow, water, light and an acceptable range of temperature, the crazy teacher sought to refine these points by suggesting that the plant could live in the fridge if the oven was too hot. Pupils were asked to take the plant to better places to live or to point to suitable potential homes. In this way the group moved towards a set of criteria for acceptable habitats for all four of the living things in question - fish, bird, mammal and plant. These criteria built upon the suggestions made by pupils on the basis of their previous experience and hopefully refined their understandings as to why life is like that. They were then used explicitly as a set of shared performance criteria in relation to the practical tasks which formed the next part of the session.

Tasks are relevant to the context in which they occur

The discussions which occurred as a result of the burlesque introduction led naturally into the next part of the session which was to involve pupils in the construction of suitable habitats for the creatures who had been subjected to the crazy teacher's calculated ineptitude. One of the intentions of this part of the session was that pupils would have a chance to practise a range of skills as part of their development towards technological competence and practical independence. From the point of view of skill acquisition alone, it would have been possible simply to require pupils to saw, drill and nail together random pieces of wood or to construct the ubiquitous match box holder as a gift for their parents. Tasks were designed, however, which would offer opportunities to exercise these and other skills within the context of the need the session had identified to construct appropriate environments for different kinds of living things.

The learning experience is coherent, relevant, purposeful and meaningful

In this way the session progressed seamlessly from checking and exercising previously gained understanding, through a phase introducing a new theoretical structure, towards a practical phase whose relevance and rationale were already established. The intention was to provide a spectrum of learning experiences which had continuity, both within the session and within the scheme of work, and which were integrated, both in terms of the structure of the particular session, using theory to inform practice in a logical progression, and in terms of subject content within the whole curriculum. Further, the session had meaning for the pupils, as had been demonstrated by their apposite and compassionate responses to the crazy teacher's life-threatening habitats and by the process of establishing shared criteria for habitats which would be kinder and more appropriate.

Tasks are clearly identified

In order to identify the practical tasks with which pupils were to engage, the class was divided into three groups and offered three different activities. Each of these involved the provision of a suitable habitat for one of the living things identified in the first part of the session. The ways in which the nature of these tasks was identified for pupils varied. It was suggested to the member of staff working with the first sub-group that a full demonstration, to completion, of the proposed activities would constitute a good introduction to the tasks for these pupils. The second group were given a verbal introduction to their task and were encouraged to look at, discuss and learn from a previously constructed habitat. The third group were simply given tools, materials and verbal instructions. It was suggested to them that they should think about other animal habitats they might have seen at home; at the homes of friends and relations or around the school in designing and building their own living space. In this way the introductions to the practical tasks were themselves differentiated according to the aptitudes of the pupils in the various groups, but, in each case, pupils gained a clear understanding of what was to be expected of them.

Planning takes account of existing skills, interests, aptitudes and experiences

The intention was to provide actual tasks appropriately differentiated according to the skills and aptitudes of a wide range of pupils. In engaging the whole pupil, including memories and experiences of family and friends, it was possible to predict that some existing interests and experiences would be brought into use in the classroom. Further, there was a clear sense in which this session had been planned to build upon concepts taught in previous weeks.

Although pupils were encouraged to form their own groupings during other sessions in the scheme of work, pupils were, on this occasion, allocated to one of three sub-groups at the planning stage. These groups were formed according to three different principles: one group was to be skills orientated, offering pupils a chance to gain new skills or to refine existing ones; a second group was to be given a problem solving activity requiring little of the participants in terms of new skills; the third group would be challenged in terms of their willingness to explore new ideas, skills and solutions. All the groups would be called upon to interact and co-operate. Individual pupils were allocated to these groups according to staff perceptions of their previous interests and achievements and priorities in terms of their current learning programmes.

The first of these groups was asked to create habitats for a handful of house plant cuttings and for the fish. Essentially pupils were encouraged to practise and to build upon existing skills in scooping (soil mixture or gravel), pouring (water), poking (planting holes for the cuttings and for the water weed) and picking up (tools in various grips and plant material, gently). The two habitats assigned to this group were deliberately simple and potentially swiftly completed. The member of staff was asked not to hurry pupils along but to let them proceed at their own pace, solving their own problems, making two or three attempts at each stage of the task if required. It was made clear that the outcome of the task was not as important as the process; that cuttings may be mangled or gravel spilled without risk of dire consequence; and that it was important to encourage all the pupils in the sub-group to participate even if it meant repeating certain aspects of the work. The intention was to enable pupils to work towards some basic, skills orientated objectives in the context of a scheme of work relating to the National Curriculum (Byers, 1992).

A second group were given the task of constructing a nest box for the bird out of pre-cut pieces of timber. Decisions about how to join the materials and which of a range of tools to use were left to the group. The thinking behind this activity was that it would not demand measuring skills or the sophisticated use of cutting tools. It would, however, require pupils to solve the problem of how to fit the available pieces together in order to make something which looked and functioned like the similar but deliberately non-identical example with which they could compare their own efforts. It was felt that this would constitute an appropriately challenging level of activity for the particular pupils allocated to this group, who had previously demonstrated a readiness to begin to tackle problem solving situations if the challenge was not too complex or multi-faceted. Again, staff were prepared to support pupils in their decisions, but deliberately set out to offer as little help as possible.

Learning is interactive - there is dialogue

The nest box building activity prompted a good deal of conversation. Words like 'roof', 'side', 'hole' and 'floor' were soon being bandied about. Suggestions were made about 'nails', 'hammers' and 'glue' and the model nest box was examined for hints about its construction. A lively debate ensued about how to assemble the available pieces and about which roles should be assigned to whom within the construction task. Staff monitored proceedings in order to guide discussions when debate threatened to degenerate into confrontation and argument. Notions about turn-taking or, conversely, about encouraging pupils to exercise previously demonstrated expertise were introduced. The activity deliberately made very few new demands upon pupils in terms of physical skills, but it certainly led them into new territory as far as their powers of communication and co-operation were concerned. It demanded interaction, leading to negotiation and ultimately a collaborative approach to the completion of the task.

There is pupil initiation, exploration and problem solving

The third group were given a much more adventurous task - to build a hutch for the rabbit. They were also given some pre-cut timber, but they had no model to work from and they did need to do some measuring and cutting in order to complete their task. The group fairly quickly put together a roof, floor and walls but baulked at the idea of making a door. They wanted something with 'windows' which would open and close. At the point at which the group threatened to disintegrate in the face of an apparently insoluble problem, a member of staff stepped in to suggest using wire mesh as a covering on a timber frame, presenting a whole new range of measuring and fixing problems. It was a pupil, however, who knew about hinges; who located some among the oddments provided and who introduced the idea of using screws, drills and screwdrivers.

Learning activities are intrinsically motivating

No externally provided rewards were used during this session. Pupils participated because they were motivated to do so either because their imaginations had been captured by the reason for the practical activities or because of the nature of the activities themselves. Those pupils who did become bored or temporarily distracted or who needed to find some quiet space away from the noise and activity were allowed to move away to the reading corner, or to walk around the periphery of the room, observing the activities of the other groups for a while. Pupils were always eventually drawn back to their tasks, either because they wished to become engaged once more or, on occasion, because their peers requested their presence for particular parts of the activity.

There is pupil self evaluation

When all the habitats were roughly completed, the groups came back together in order to look at one another's work. At this stage, the whole class discussed refinements which would improve the habitats or which would render them hospitable in the long term. Thus a pot of fish food was located and placed beside the tank after pupils had added a sprinkle or two to the water. A watering can was filled for the benefit of the plant cuttings and their growing medium moistened. Straw was added to the nesting box and to the rabbit hutch which was also furnished with dishes for water and food. Photographs were taken of the sub-groups gathered around their creations and the objects themselves were arranged for permanent display by the pupils as a form of real object recording of the activities in which they had been engaged that day (see chapters 5 and 11). A final summation of the session's activities reminded pupils of the criteria for appropriate habitats which they had established at the start of the session and invited them to apply these standards to their newly created habitats.

Conclusion

The intention of this chapter has been to put some illustrative flesh upon the bones of learning theory. It has certainly not set out to establish a new dogma for 'good practice' or the 'right' way to teach pupils with learning difficulties. One of the main contentions of the theory of effective learning is that pupils themselves learn in different ways, using a variety of individual learning styles. Teaching approaches, if they are to be effective, should accommodate and encourage this variety through a balanced range of learning opportunities. It would be possible, therefore, to generate a wholly different set of examples to illustrate the principles which provide the structure of this chapter - examples which would provide effective learning opportunities for different pupils in different learning contexts. In acknowledging this reality, this chapter has described a range of different kinds of learning taking place within the same session, some of it directed, some of it exploratory; some of it individual, some of it collaborative. All of the learning described accords with the broad principles of effective learning and provides opportunities for personal and social development while ensuring access to the content of the curriculum.

Chapter Ten

Devising and Implementing a Cross-curricular School Recording System - a Case Study

Sue Chesworth

All record keeping takes place within a context

A record keeping system cannot be developed in isolation from the situation in which it is designed to function. When I was assigned the task of developing a whole school recording system it was imperative that I reflect upon the situation in which that system was to operate. The school in which I work is a secondary school for students with severe learning difficulties. The school caters for students within the age range of eleven to nineteen years. It is divided into two departments, the lower school, which caters for students aged eleven to sixteen years, and a further education department, which caters for students of sixteen to nineteen years. The further education department had adopted a subject based method of curriculum delivery when it was opened in the early 1980s. This had proved to be an effective method of curriculum delivery for this age group. In 1990 the lower school changed from a class based method of curriculum delivery similar to a mainstream primary school model to the subject based secondary model which was successfully being applied within the further education department.

My task, to devise a whole school recording system, started in September 1991. As one would anticipate, the effects of the changed method of curriculum delivery upon staff in the lower school was quite considerable. They had to modify the organisation of their teaching. The changes also had quite a divisive effect upon collaborative teaching.

Although the majority of staff were not subject specialists, they suddenly found themselves in a position of being nominated as the school specialist and in some instances the sole deliverer of certain curriculum areas. The effect was that staff tended to withdraw into their curriculum area in order to develop their curriculum expertise. Great concern was expressed that students were being denied the quality of individual attention which had been evident under the class based system. They were now being taught by a large number of staff who were not familiar with the students' specific individual needs. There was also concern that staff did not know what was being taught in other curriculum areas. There was no means of monitoring the whole curriculum which students were receiving. It was felt that under the previous system the class teacher had thorough knowledge of each student in his class.

Within this situation staff were developing their own subject specific recording systems and there were relics of recording systems which had existed under the class based system. So it could be said that I have endeavoured to develop a recording system which serves the needs of this particular situation, out of the ashes of the old system and the nervous spring shoots of the new organisation.

The development of collaborative record keeping

My task started when the staff were in the aftermath of a considerable change in teaching arrangements. It was particularly important not to create any unnecessary additional change. In order to assess the recording procedures which were currently in use I carried out a recording audit (see chapter 4). This involved the staff in completing a questionnaire relating to their personal recording activities. The results of the questionnaire demonstrated that the majority of staff were using a personal recording system which recorded individual students' responses to lessons. Many staff also set subject specific aims. This information, combined with staff desire to know what was being taught in other curriculum areas, provided the impetus to run a pilot cross-curricular project.

It was agreed that the core subject teachers would plan and implement a cross-curricular project for four weeks during November 1991. The relevant teachers met and went through a process of brainstorming, negotiating what their particular curriculum area would cover and agreeing a common recording format. The planning and response sheets used were based upon those illustrated by Lawson (1992) in *Practical Record Keeping in Special Schools*. Each student involved in the pilot had a cross-curricular aim, usually of a social nature.

Alongside this the subject teachers identified subject specific aims.

The evaluation questionnaire which followed the pilot showed that the staff involved considered the collaborative planning to be useful and the process of planning and recording to be worthy of development within school. However there were considerable concerns expressed about the amount of time which could be needed to plan a similar project if more staff were to become involved. As the pilot had been a voluntary commitment, there was fear that such planning and collaboration would be expected to continue to take place on a voluntary basis rather than in directed time. Although the staff involved had experienced the potential benefits of cross-curricular planning, time was the burning issue which needed to be addressed.

The pilot study had taken place in the autumn term of 1991. In the latter part of the spring term 1992, I invited any interested members of staff to plan a cross-curricular project for the following term, summer 1992. At this stage staff were still attending planning meetings voluntarily. To my surprise, the whole lower school staff, plus a couple of staff from the further education department, agreed to take part in the project. They emphasised that it was as a trial and that they would not be prepared to give of their own time for future projects. With this in mind, I organised four thirty minute meetings, keeping a tight hold upon the meetings to keep them task orientated. As with the pilot study, teachers used the same planning procedure, planning sheets and recording sheets. For this project, staff recorded subject specific information only. No specific cross-curricular aims were set. The project ran according to plan for ten weeks of the summer term and was duly evaluated at its conclusion. The evaluation showed a favourable response to the cross-curricular approach and a willingness to continue using the method devised. This was with the proviso that two hours directed time be allocated for planning the next project. The individual response sheets were proving useful and provided a common format on which staff could continue to record in a manner with which they were familiar.

The saga has a happy ending in that during the autumn term the staff were given two hours directed time in which to plan a project for the spring term 1993.

Implementation of collaborative recording

The previous section described the development of content based record keeping. However the staff had highlighted two other dimensions of record keeping which needed to be addressed. They were as follows:

- recording related to the particular needs of students with profound and multiple learning difficulties;
- the recording of aims and achievements for personal and social education - something which had been an integral part of the class teacher's role under the previous class based system.

The problem relating to students with profound and multiple learning difficulties was addressed by the implementation of yet another pilot study. In January 1992 the pastoral teachers of five students with profound and multiple learning difficulties identified cross-curricular aims for the students in their pastoral groups. These were written on an individual response sheet like those used for subject specific recording (Lawson, 1992). Each student had a personal folder in which the individual response sheet was housed. As the students selected for this pilot were all wheelchair users it was agreed that the folders could be carried on the back of their wheelchairs to the various subject lessons. At a general staff meeting, all staff were informed about the pilot. They were asked to use the cross-curricular individual response sheets to record any achievements relating to the identified aims. The hope was that a system would evolve for recording the specific aims and achievements relating to this particular group of students. The pilot was evaluated by the ubiquitous questionnaire to staff. The outcome showed that staff approved of the ideas and principles behind this type of recording but many of them confessed to having insufficient time in their lessons to allow for the regular use of cross-curricular recording sheets. The heartening news was that in principle they agreed this type of recording for this group of students.

The problem of personal and social aims for all students was addressed in a slightly different way. There was a pilot scheme!

Concurrent with the development of a whole school recording there was a change in organisation of staff meetings. Part of this change was the emergence of meetings devoted to student needs. These meetings involved departmental pastoral staff. The function of the meetings was to discuss students' general progress and specifically set cross-curricular personal and social aims for each student. The student need meetings were usually scheduled for approximately two meetings each half term. Four students were usually discussed at each meeting. This was a rolling programme which enabled each student's progress to be reviewed approximately once a year. Stemming from these meetings the need arose to create a common format to record the aims set for each student at the relevant student need meeting. The individual response sheet being used in the other areas of recording conveniently fitted the bill.

Consequently each student has cross-curricular personal and social aims which are collaboratively set and recorded on the common format individual response sheet.

Both the systems which I have described above are very much in their infancy, although developing. The folders for students with profound and multiple learning difficulties have become an everyday part of school life and now also encompass multi-disciplinary information such as the recording of epileptic fits or positioning of non-ambulant students so that staff know whether the student has been in her standing frame all day. Each member of staff has a personal copy of the cross-curricular personal and social aims sheets on which he may record in preparation for the following review.

To conclude this section, the school now has a developing three-pronged recording system comprising the following elements: subject specific recording, recording in relation to cross-curricular personal and social aims and recording specific to students with profound and multiple learning difficulties. This type of recording is designed to support the delivery of a subject based curriculum in a school for students with severe learning difficulties.

Common principles

It may sound wonderful to have developed such a sophisticated school recording system. However, the sobering fact is that no recording system is effective unless it produces the information which it was designed to produce. The reality is that although staff have been very positive in their initial evaluations of the system, I know that not all staff use the designated sheets in the appropriate manner. In practice, recording systems must be simple, economical and user friendly in order to be used in the long term. In the present educational climate, it is imperative that teachers maintain comprehensive records. For experienced, long serving teachers the habit of thorough record keeping does not always come naturally. Teachers tend to see record keeping as something which must be done in their own time after the lesson. By the very nature of a special school community, unexpected things frequently happen! These unpredictable events often distract the teacher from his good intentions to spend a lunch time completing the morning's records. Therefore a backlog develops and memories fade. The recording inevitably loses accuracy and relevance. In order to overcome this situation there must be a shift in the teacher's perception of the role of record keeping.

The recording which I have described in this chapter is formative record keeping. In that sense it is an integral part of teaching. Once this situation has been recognised then teachers may begin to accept that it is acceptable, even positively praiseworthy, to spend five minutes at the end of each lesson completing records. In some cases it will be appropriate to include students in this process by consulting them on how they felt they coped with the demands of the lesson (see chapters 5 and 11). It cannot be stressed too strongly that it requires a considerable shift in teachers' perceptions in order for this attitude to prevail.

The staff have felt comfortable with the organisation of the recording system because it has gradually built upon existing practice within the school. It is important that staff feel familiar with the system and have some ownership of its development. As mentioned previously, there is no use in having a recording system which is not being used. As it is classroom teachers who are being required to use the system, they must have ownership and influence over the implementation of the system.

Finally, the function of the recording system which has evolved at this particular school is formative in nature. It emphasises information generating, particularly for the benefit of students with profound and multiple learning difficulties. It also generates information sharing and the development of commonly negotiated themes and goals.

Conclusion

Although the title of this case study implies that it is specifically related to developing a whole school recording system, it is evident from the material presented that recording cannot evolve in isolation from the situation it is serving. The relationship between recording and many other aspects of school organisation is an interesting and complex one.

Initially I described an organisational change which the lower school staff had experienced. In some respects the recording system was developed in order to co-ordinate some of the effects of that change. It represented an attempt to collate activities and student progress throughout the school. This was the aim but on reflection the results have perhaps been more far reaching. Although in some respects the recording system represented an attempt to consolidate one major change, the result has been to create a need for further innovation. The change which is now being required of teachers is a change in perception and attitude. The responses to each set of evaluation questionnaires was favourable in principle. Staff agreed with the methods of collaborative planning, common recording format, the common recording of progress in terms of personal and social development and the achievements of students with profound and multiple learning difficulties. Despite this agreement in principle, there remained a common resistance in attitude towards the various activities.

However it is possible to look more closely at the type of change which the recording system is asking the staff to make. Collaborative planning requires staff to share ideas and negotiate curriculum content. With the type of class based teaching which existed previously there had not been the need to share information, However, under the subject based system the staff themselves had identified this need. Despite identifying the need themselves and appreciating the benefits of collaborative planning they still resisted the required change. The same type of resistance was expressed towards the recording of cross-curricular achievements for students with profound and multiple learning difficulties. Despite agreeing in principle, staff found it difficult to complete the necessary forms consistently. This highlights another change which the staff were being required to make. They were being asked to adapt their perceptions of the role of recording. Many teachers could not accept that recording achievements could become an integral part of each lesson. They felt that recording was something which must be done very much as an afterthought. This is a fundamental change which will take time to become a common part of practice, particularly if the teacher is experienced and is used to using well established personal procedures.

The maintenance of regular recording requires self discipline on the part of the teacher. With teachers being required to be increasingly accountable, effective, up to date record keeping is essential. Maintaining this degree of self discipline requires commitment to the process in which staff are involved. In many instances experienced teachers have functioned apparently adequately with piecemeal recording systems and have not acknowledged the need to modify their methods. They have little real commitment to the present emphasis on record keeping and its integral role within the education process. With this discrepancy in commitment it is little wonder that they find it hard to apply the self discipline which is necessary in order to complete the required documentation.

The notion of time management has been highlighted within this case study. There is a need for time to be allocated specifically for the purpose of planning. This final point can serve to unify many other points which have been raised in this concluding section. The staff's response to the development of a whole school recording system has reflected many of the issues that are concerning teachers at the time of the case study. Teachers feel that they are being required to undertake extra tasks with no extra time in which to perform them. Many of the changes which ensued from the Education Reform Act (DES, 1988), such as accountability or curriculum content, have sent lasting ripples through the profession. These ripples have produced some resistance. The resistance can be seen in microcosm in the teachers' resistance to the implementation of some of the recording which was being required of them.

Finally I would like to reiterate that the implementation of a recording system is a complex process upon which many forces are brought to bear. As the influencing factors are constantly changing so the recording system must be sufficiently flexible to incorporate those changes yet at the same time remain constant to basic, commonly agreed principles. In the instance described in this case study I feel that staff have identified some commonly agreed principles but must continue to work collaboratively in order to implement those principles in a manner which is comfortable and which meets the needs of national criteria.

Chapter Eleven

Pupil Participation in their own Records of Achievement

Joy Hardwick and Peter Rushton

With acknowledgements to:
- *staff and pupils at Wren Spinney School, Kettering;*
- *members of the Northamptonshire working party for Records of Achievement in special schools, who helped to develop some of the materials described in this chapter;*
- *Margaret Jones, of Northamptonshire Inspectorate and Advisory Service, for advice on action planning.*

Introduction

This chapter will explore pupil participation in recording their own achievements and will consider the issue of finding means of communication by which pupils with learning difficulties can make such a contribution. The chapter will look at some strategies for enhancing recording devices already used in schools. These will include use of photographs and video, action planning techniques and the use of concept keyboards to assist in self-assessment processes.

Since the advent of the Education Reform Act (DES, 1988), regulations have come into force governing procedures for recording and reporting student achievement and attainment. Regulations set out the duties of local education authorities, governing bodies and head-teachers in ensuring that these procedures are adhered to.

The regulations determine a focus upon the recording and reporting of achievement and attainment within the assessment structure for National Curriculum subjects. In schools for pupils with learning difficulties, there is a tradition of using recording and reporting procedures which reflect whole pupil achievement, with academic achievement as a part of this. School staff should be looking at how their established good practice is meeting the regulations before trying to set up new systems, as any interpretation which loses the spirit of enhancing existing good practice is detrimental to both students and staff.

Staff in schools for pupils with learning difficulties can be assured that much good practice to be found in mainstream education derives from work among pupils with special educational needs, detailed recording of achievement being a good example of this. However, as school leavers must now legally have a Record of Achievement, there has been an increase in anxiety about its implementation. In some instances, it is seen as just another legal requirement, something to be done and presented to the student when they leave school. There is a danger that this element of obligation will lead to teacher dominated Records of Achievement for pupils with learning difficulties.

Schools need to develop a Records of Achievement policy which co-ordinates the processes of assessment, recording and reporting. Staff, students, parents and governors should work together. Recording of achievement should become an integral part of curriculum planning and classroom delivery (DES, 1991).

School staff need to generate a positive attitude to recording of achievement as a whole and, in particular, to student involvement in the recording processes. The value of a final Records of Achievement document will surely be increased for the student if there is a feeling of ownership, of having participated in its production through processes of self assessment (Lawson, 1992).

Communication for pupils with learning difficulties

It is important that pupils with learning difficulties contribute to their own Records of Achievement in order that the records reflect their own values and preferences. There may be considerable difficulties in enabling these pupils to make such a contribution, particularly if they have limited speech and writing skills. For such pupils, the challenge may be seen as finding an appropriate means of communication with which they can express their own values and preferences (see chapter 7). Technology may be used in order to overcome some physical difficulties (see chapter 8). For pupils with learning difficulties, the methods used need to be carefully considered so that they allow genuine choices without becoming so cumbersome that the mechanics of choice start to dominate the process.

Once a suitable means of communication has been found to enable students to contribute to their own Records of Achievement, the next step is to ensure that the method of communicating is their own. Many pupils with learning difficulties are very suggestible and it is easy for staff, even unwittingly, to over-influence decisions and choices made by pupils. We have noticed that many such pupils, when offered a choice expressed verbally, will always plump for the last item mentioned. For example, 'Do you want red, blue or green?' will be answered by 'green', whereas 'Do you want green, blue or red?' will be answered by 'red'. Others might be excessively influenced by tone of voice, with staff 'highlighting' the answers which they want or expect. If pupils are asked to select favourite activities by choosing picture cards, are all cards equally accessible?

It is important that pupils are offered opportunities to make genuine choices throughout their time in school in order that the processes of choice become familiar to them; that they be encouraged not only to initiate acts of choosing but also to give some consideration to the results of their choices. It is, therefore, preferable to involve pupils in their own Records of Achievement as early as possible in their school careers. Where symbolic systems of recording are to be used, pupils need time to become familiar with these. This familiarity with symbols and procedures will, hopefully, reduce the pupil's dependency on staff intervention in their Records of Achievement.

Pupils with profound and multiple learning difficulties present particular challenges and the difficulties associated with finding an appropriate method of communication for these pupils can be considerable. Many schools have used photographs, video tapes or sensory objects (for pupils with dual sensory impairment) to record responses to activities, thereby offering evidence of progress, achievement and student preferences (see chapter 7).

Approaches to Records of Achievement with pupils with learning difficulties

Photographs and video

The majority of schools have long had a tradition of photographic displays. For example, photographs of the rugby and netball teams, with results printed alongside, or of the participants in school plays or concerts, adorned the entrances to many mainstream schools and were regarded as an important element in determining first impressions of the school. Advances in technology have made photographic techniques much more available and schools have tended to use photographs in increasing abundance for all types of display work. In the past few years, video recording has also become a common practice in most schools.

If photographs and video recordings are to be a part of a school's Records of Achievement implementation policy, their role must be determined by agreed criteria. In the early days of Records of Achievement development, a 'scrapbook' element appeared, with the use of many photographs (recording various activities) and a final Records of Achievement document, resembling a photograph album, being produced for presentation to the student on leaving school. While this had value, its usefulness as a record of achievement can be enhanced by adherence to a more stuctured policy towards the use of photographic evidence.

A photograph of Lee sitting upright on a horse might act as a record of an experience, a memento to show that Lee went horse riding. The same photograph might also be used as evidence that Lee sat upright on the horse unaided for the first time after weeks of practice. The comment alongside the photograph increases its value as a record. Its value increases further if the comment is part of the pupil's self assessment. Did Lee help to choose which photographs went into his Record of Achievement? If so, why was this photograph important to him? Photographs with comments written for the pupil by members of staff can form a useful biographical record, but comments provided, where possible, by the pupil will form an autobiographical record and have greater validity.

In practice, many teachers use their own cameras to take photographs. This can lead to an over abundance of shots of special events such as outings, with less emphasis on routine classroom events. A school or department policy is helpful here. This might entail having a camera with film readily available to record significant achievements, evidence or progress whenever these occur. If one camera is used consistently for this purpose, pupils will not have to wait too long for films to be processed, particularly if that camera is a Polaroid.

The usefulness of video as a tool for recording achievement can also be enhanced through a school policy. Video records of special events such as concerts or outings are of value, but the achievements of individual pupils can get lost within a mass of footage. In addition to these, a school might consider periodically recording particular skills (for instance, feeding, fine motor skills or swimming) for groups of pupils. Good editing helps here, as does the facility to superimpose the date on video footage. Some schools may not be able to afford sophisticated editing equipment, but where suitable editing facilities exist, there is a strong argument for each pupil having their own video tape as an ongoing Record of Achievements, particularly for pupils with profound and multiple learning difficulties.

Pupils usually enjoy watching themselves on video. Some might be encouraged to comment on what progress they can see in their own abilities through watching themselves on video recordings taken over a period of time. This could be used to aid the development of self appraisal skills.

Ready availability of the equipment is as important with video as with still cameras. It is rare that the video camera will be running when a pupil achieves something for the first time (the first step unaided or the first strokes in the pool), but a recording made at the next opportunity will still have value.

Photographic and video equipment can go some way towards providing a means of communication for pupils with profound and multiple learning difficulties. If we value this 'voice', then it is desirable that we learn to use the equipment proficiently. A school will benefit from devoting some time on a staff training day to improving photographic and video techniques.

Using a concept keyboard to record achievements

Many schools have used computers with concept keyboards to enable pupils to participate in writing their own Records of Achievement. Schools in Northamptonshire have used the 'Prompt/Writer' word processing package. Staff from several schools for pupils with learning difficulties worked together to produce a standard format which can then be added to in order to produce an overlay for recording a particular area of achievement.

Using the 'Prompt/Writer' software, it is then quite easy to make customised overlays to suit particular activities or areas of achievement. In the following example, figure 11.1, the squares in the first column and the last two columns form the standard overlay format with the other squares being subject specific.

By pressing the appropriate squares on the concept keyboard overlay, the student can type out statements relating to their own preferences and achievements. For instance:

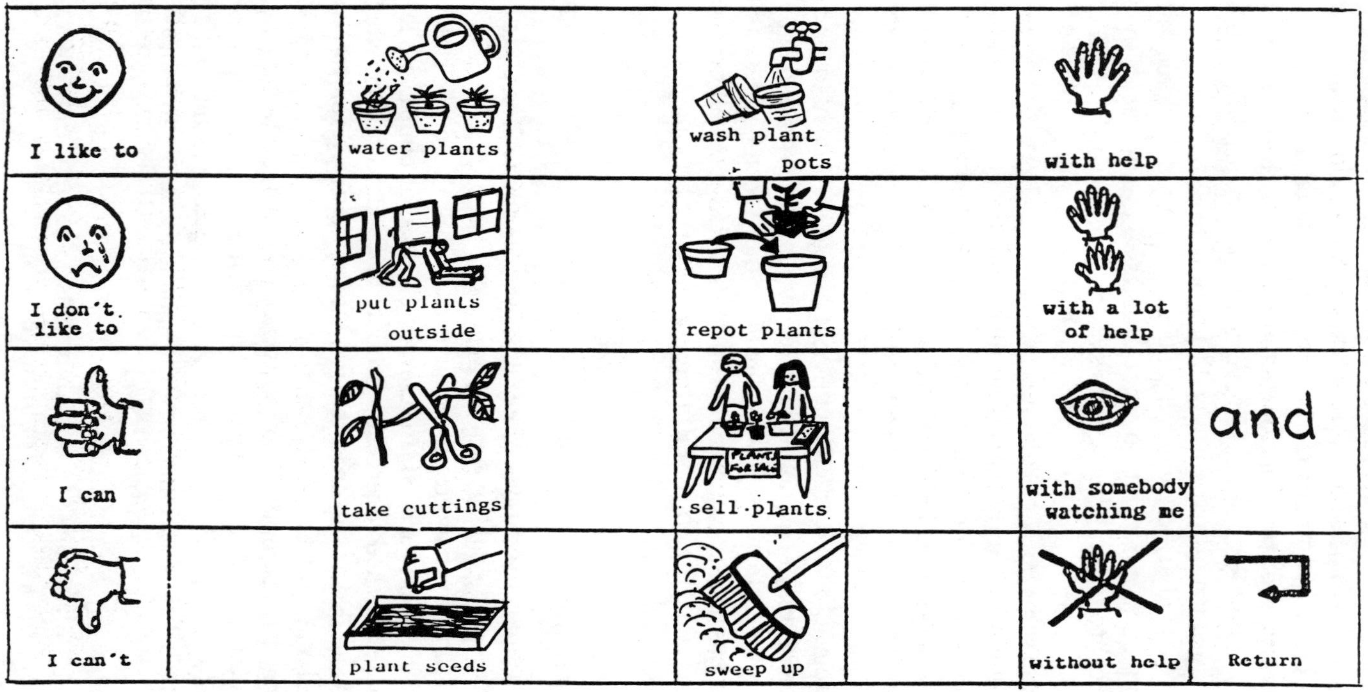

Figure 11.1: Concept keyboard overlay

> I like to plant seeds
> I can water plants without help

The use of a standard format has certain advantages:

- Schools are able to exchange overlays as the pupils in each school are familiar with the same format;
- Pupils get used to working in the same left to right manner and become familiar with the positions and meanings of the symbols used in the standard format.

Some pupils with learning difficulties are able to use this system of recording with little assistance. For others, however, the structuring of achievement statements into sentences creates difficulties. For some of these pupils, a modified approach to using these concept keyboard overlays gives access to self recording. These pupils are expected only to pick out the pictures for the activities which they liked best or feel they have achieved. The record of achievement, prepared with assistance, might read:

> Peter has been doing gardening. He was able to do these things:
>
> > water plants
> > wash plant pots
> > sweep up
>
> He did all these things with some help.
>
> The words in the box have been chosen by Peter
>
> using a picture overlay.

This way of using the material offers a reduced level of student participation, but does open up its use to a wider group of pupils.

There are several shortcomings to this method of recording achievements.

- It works best when the overlays are related to a particular lesson or activity and when the recording takes place immediately after the activity. This means that the equipment has to be readily available (not always the case). Setting up can be time consuming.
- It takes time for the students to become familiar with the system.

They require a lot of assistance at first, which detracts from the independence of their input. The hardest part is deciding how much help they require to achieve tasks. Sometimes, however, the process of discussion which has gone on while completing the recording exercise is valuable in itself.

- Though some symbols are common to all overlays, the pictures used to represent activities are not part of a standard system of symbols and it is difficult to tie them in with a wider scheme of work. Where schools use Makaton or Rebus symbols in other contexts, it would be preferable to link these to systems of recording.

- The greatest drawback to this system is that the students only get a written Record of Achievement. Pictures are used to produce the record, but the written record is often meaningless to the student without somebody to read it back to them.

In the light of some of these shortcomings, some schools are now moving to a similar use of concept keyboards using 'From Pictures to Words' software as opposed to 'Prompt/Writer'. Many of the symbols used in this package are similar to standard Makaton symbols already in use in many schools. The main advantage of using 'From Pictures to Words' is that the printed statements of achievement can be accompanied by picture symbols, enabling more pupils to understand their content.

For example, a concept keyboard overlay may look like figure 11.2. This may enable a pupil to produce a record similar to figure 11.3, with picture symbols to aid the pupil's own understanding of the record. Schools with access to scanners will be able to include photographs in the printout as well.

Selecting and editing

Throughout each school year, a pupil can acquire a great deal of evidence of their experiences and achievements. The Records of Achievement policy should have formative and summative elements with processes of selection and editing taking place at regular intervals. A model for a school's Records of Achievement process could be as shown in figure 11.4.

At the end of each unit of work, there is a process of negotiation between teacher and pupil to determine what goes into a yearly evidence folder. The folder is also used to hold evidence of other achievements.

SLD RECORDS OF ACHIEVEMENT PROJECT

FILENAME: _P.E.1_

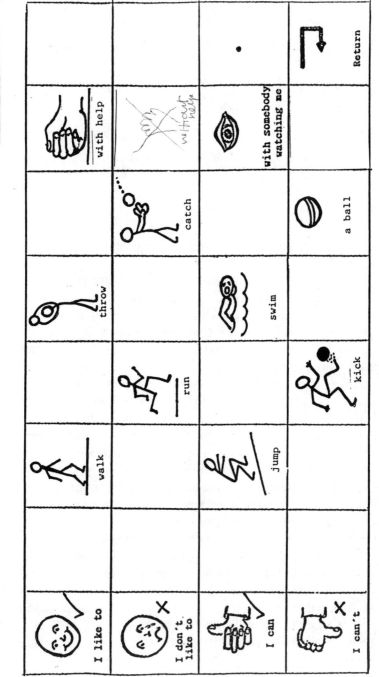

Wren Spinney School

Figure 11.2: Concept keyboard overlay with symbols

I can catch

a ball.

I can jump.

Figure 11.3: Printed Record of Achievement sheet with symbols

Any event or achievement which is significant to the pupil should be recorded.

As pupils and staff will have to be selective about what is retained in the evidence folder, decisions will have to be made about what happens to other material which does not make it through the selection process. The pupils may wish to take it home or it could be thrown away. Ideally, the pupils themselves will make these decisions. It is quite natural for a pupil who is particularly proud of an achievement to want to take evidence of this achievement home to show to family and friends as soon as possible. Inclusion of the evidence in an evidence folder may well be of a lower priority to the pupil. This conflict of interests can, in some instances, be avoided by, for instance, making copies of certificates or photographs so that one copy can go home while another goes into the folder. It is also important to develop the pupil's sense of ownership of the folder and to develop a feeling of pride in its contents. For instance, during pastoral tutorials a member of staff could periodically go through the evidence folder with the pupil, discussing its contents and praising the achievements recorded within.

At the end of each year, the yearly evidence folder provides material for a summative Records of Achievement document. Again, the editing process should involve negotiation between staff and pupils. This could be done either at the end of the academic year or at the time of the pupil's annual review. When pupils are encouraged to contribute to their own annual reviews, the evidence folder should become a tool to help them to do this.

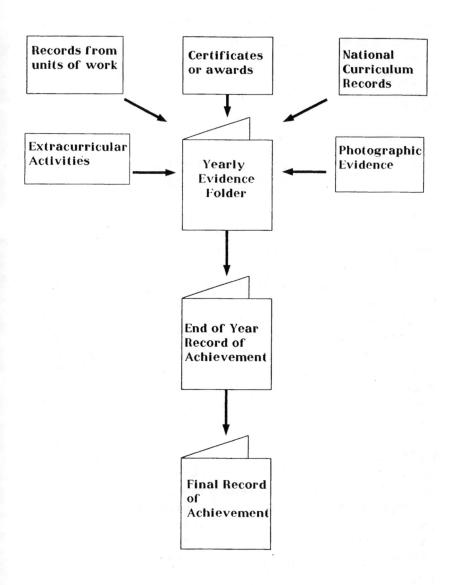

Figure 11.4: The Records of Achievement process

A final Records of Achievement document is presented to the pupils when they leave school. The annual Records of Achievement documents from previous years and the evidence folder from the pupil's final year in school will be edited to provide material for the final Records of Achievement document. As with previous stages, it is important to involve the pupils in this refining process as far as possible. It is their record and the achievements which mean most to them should take precedence.

Assessment as part of the curriculum

In order to help pupils to make self assessments for their records of achievement, they should be regularly encouraged to make assessments of their own and other people's abilities within a variety of curriculum activities. For example, students might conduct a survey of the favoured activities of school staff, things they enjoy doing and don't enjoy doing, and things they feel they are good at. Looking at other people's strengths and preferences offers one road to developing assessment skills which might then be applied to the student's own abilities and preferences.

Another approach is to use T.V. programmes as a basis for work on assessment. Pupils might watch an episode of *Neighbours* together with follow up work on the particular qualities of the characters in the programme. This could form part of the curriculum for personal and social education

When planning units of work for pupils with learning difficulties, review and evaluation elements can be built in to encourage self assessment at regular intervals. For instance, in physical education, pupils might be encouraged to assess their own achievements against established checklists such as those provided by 'Ten Steps' for athletics or the B.A.G.A. awards for gymnastics. Evaluation exercises need not be lengthy or elaborate, but should encourage the pupils to think about their own involvement in an activity. The example (figure 11.5) shows a pupil evaluation form used at the end of each of a series of geography lessons called 'Learning About Maps'.

Action planning

Action planning approaches to the curriculum can be used to develop assessment skills. Prior to commencing a curriculum activity, the teacher and pupil negotiate realistic and achievable targets, with an

LEARNING ABOUT MAPS
PUPIL EVALUATION FORM

Pupil name. DAVID

Lesson no. 6

Did you enjoy the lesson ? yes

What did you enjoy most ? Finding places on maps

Were there bits of the lesson you didn't enjoy ? reading THE small words ON THE MAPS

What was the lesson about ? maps

places where I was born

Which activities were best in today's lesson ? i liked The mazes

Who did you enjoy working with ?

Mr rose AND SARAH

Figure 11.5: Pupil evaluation form

agreed set of rewards built in. At the (
work, the pupils should be involved in
Have the targets been reached? Shared :
defined from the outset will help the
decision (see chapter 9). Some schools I
of another member of staff acting as
discuss the work with the pupils at the
stages.

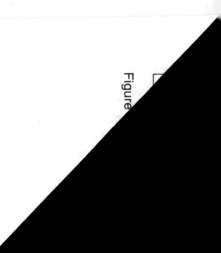

142

Figure 11.6 shows an action planning record sheet introduced to a group of pupils with learning difficulties. Pupils helped to design the form themselves. The words 'helper' and 'checker' were their own. They were allowed to choose their own checker from amongst the school staff and negotiated their own rewards.

Name *Simon*

Project redecorate the dolls house

Targets

May 11 *1 Rub with sand paper*
         2 Choose the blue paint
         3 Choose the wallpaper pattern
         4 Help glue the wallpaper on
         5 Redecorate the dolls house

Helper

Sarah, Joy, Simon will help himself

Rewards

For 1 target *biscuit with drink in the afternoon*
    2 targets *sticker*
    3 targets *extra swimming*
    4 targets *watch the video or listen to tapes of "Joseph"*
    5 targets *TRIP TO MCDONALDS*

11.6: Pupil action plan

Module *"Simple Cookery Plus"*   Term *Spring '93*

Name   *Peter*   **School** *Wren Spinney*

Targets

1. To put ingredients in a bowl in the right order for making a cake, following instructions given by another student (David)

2. Match bags to biscuits according to size for the biscuit stall

Rewards

1. A certificate of achievement for helping to make the cake

2. To choose one bag of biscuits for himself

Tutor Signature *J. Pritchard* **Student Signature** _____
Date *5 May 1993*   **Date**   *8 May 1993*

Review
Peter enjoyed the module. He worked with David on cakes and achieved Target 1 after three weeks. Peter was able to match the largest biscuits with the correct bags

Peter was presented with a certificate of achievement.

Tutors Signature *J. Pritchard* **Students Signature** _____

Date   *1st July 1993*   **Date**   *1st July 1993*

Figure 11.7: Negotiated target and review sheet

Figure 11.7 is a further example of a record sheet with targets and rewards agreed prior to a curriculum activity. It relates to a module of work on cookery which involved making cakes and biscuits and setting up a stall in order to sell them. Where pupils have limited reading skills, symbols could be incorporated into this type of record sheet.

Conclusion

The extent to which pupils with learning difficulties are able to contribute to their own Records of Achievement will vary greatly according to the nature of their individual needs. Whilst recognising that no single approach is likely to be suitable for all pupils with learning difficulties, this chapter has suggested some ways in which pupil self assessment can be accessed at a number of different levels. Staff who try out some of the approaches mentioned above, such as the use of information technology, video or action planning, will be able to take these as a starting point when trying to find appropriate means of communication for pupil self assessment and will be encouraged to develop their own strategies. We have emphasised two general principles relating to Records of Achievement. Firstly, that the records will have greater value and more meaning if the students have been encouraged to contribute to them as fully as possible and, secondly, that Records of Achievement should be regarded as an integral part of the curriculum as opposed to a separate activity in order to fulfil statutory obligations.

Note: *Prompt/Writer* software is produced by Special Needs Software Centre, National Council for Educational Technology.

From Pictures to Words software is published by Widgit Software, 102 Radford Road, Leamington Spa, Warwicks.

Chapter Twelve

Advocacy: not just another Subject

Jan Tyne

It may seem out of place to have a chapter about advocacy included in a book which is primarily concerned with highlighting innovative classroom practice and teaching methods. I believe however, that the inclusion of a discussion on advocacy is relevant and important, since much of what is taught and the teaching methods used, especially in schools for pupils with learning difficulties, depends greatly on the assumptions that the school staff make about their pupils and their place in the world.

In the following chapter an attempt is made to address some of the issues that surface during any discussion about advocacy. Issues and questions like: What is advocacy? Are there different forms of advocacy? When and why is it needed? But above all, I hope to demonstrate that advocacy should not be thought of as a subject to be taught like maths or science with its own timetable slot.

What is advocacy?

Advocacy means speaking up for, or pleading on behalf of, someone or an issue. When it concerns a person the purpose is to safeguard that person's interests and rights, for example, from abuse, exploitation or neglect, persuading service providers to provide a better service. When it concerns an issue, advocacy would benefit anyone affected by that issue rather than particular individuals.

Advocacy makes demands on people. It requires vigour and vehemence, commitment and loyalty. It is not a comfortable hat to wear and for the person who chooses to act as an advocate, inevitably there will be a personal cost in terms of time, stress, inconvenience, money and emotion. Taking on the role of advocate is not a soft option, but a challenge that requires people to examine their own values and commitments. Indeed it is said that 'if it is too easy then it probably isn't advocacy.'

Effective advocacy requires a minimal conflict of interest, so that advocates can feel sufficiently free and independent to say, honestly and without fear, what needs to be said and what needs to be done.

Why advocacy is needed

History has shown that injustice can take many forms and has existed in every age and culture. History has also shown that where injustice exists there will be people who, though not personally threatened by it, are prepared to respond by standing up, speaking out and taking action alongside or on behalf of victims of injustice. This is the general nature of advocacy.

Society's first response to people who need extra support, perhaps because of a learning disability, mental illness, or physical disability, has been to separate them from their immediate community and congregate them together, creating special schools, day centres, hostels. This gives little opportunity to build networks of friends and colleagues with whom one can share celebrations or ask for help.

For most of us there is very little that we can achieve alone. We all rely on others for support. None of us is born with all the necessary skills at our disposal to enable us to become sociable beings. We have to learn these skills by mixing with different people in many different situations - at school, college or work and in our social lives.

Keith

I would like you to know about Keith, nearing the end of his school career, facing an uncertain future as childhood finishes, with no clear picture of what will lie beyond school. A group of us met to think, with Keith, about what could lie ahead. We tried to bring together everyone who knew him well. There were only four of us, all of us paid to be there, none of us claiming to have known him for more than a few years. We were drawn to think of his past, of the people who had moved in and out of his life briefly - teachers, social workers, nurses, volunteers and the three sets of people he had known as 'mum and dad'.

Keith's life had been circumscribed by three settings: his residential unit, where he lived with twelve others; the blue bus that picked him up each school day; and the school itself. The documents of Keith's life told us little beyond the various tests and medications, the occasions he's had accidents or hurt others.

Picture a typical Friday morning: school assembly had just finished, everyone was there - pupils, staff, visitors and the local vicar. There was a lot of hustle and bustle and the youngest children and wheelchair users were being ushered out. The senior pupils were busily stacking the chairs, the vicar had been invited for coffee. At that moment a woman, dressed in a blue nurse's uniform, pushed her way into the hall, against the flow of the children and staff. 'Where's Keith?' she called. She was holding a dish with a syringe, phial and cotton wool. 'We forgot to give him his injection this morning - short staffed - the bus came early - only one person on duty. Keith wouldn't eat his cornflakes' - the excuses came thick and fast.

She promptly rushed over to Keith, and started to pull up his sleeve. Keith had just got up from his chair. He is not steady on his feet, he can't see too well. Several pairs of hands pushed him down again. Unceremoniously the injection was given in public, with no preparation or explanation to Keith. Rather meekly, one member of staff protested: 'There's a medical room next door,' but to no avail. The act was swiftly done, the woman disappeared.

Meanwhile Keith was angry, protesting, shouting, spitting, resorting to the actions that he knows gets everyone's attention. He sat down and refused to move. He had to be cajoled and physically manhandled to his feet by several school staff. He was marched, almost dragged, from the hall so that the next PE lesson could begin.

How on earth could such an event happen? Staff in schools for pupils with learning difficulties are caring, considerate people. It's in the nature of the job. Yet they all knew that Keith gets very agitated if events occur too quickly with no explanation. They all knew that he had poor eyesight. They all knew that there was a medical room next door, as did the nurse from his residential unit. Then why did they choose to ignore all that? On the face of it, Keith's 'rights' appear to have been of no consequence. Why did no-one speak up forcibly for Keith?

Susan

Then there is Susan's story. Susan has a compulsive habit of inflicting serious injuries to her face and head, causing everyone who works with her considerable anguish and distress. She is a complicated person. The reason for her 'challenging behaviour' is not obvious. She has had this 'problem' ever since she started school. The staff tried all ways they could think of to stop her hurting herself. Eventually they were driven to wholly illegal but desperate measures. Susan had the sleeves of her jumper tied together.

Apart from the gross infringment of Susan's rights as a person, the consequence of the restriction of her hands was that she had no way to protect herself if she fell. Further, Susan found speaking very difficult but she could understand Makaton and made attempts to sign. Now her only means of communication was denied. Susan's story is long and involved, but it was only when someone at last had the courage to speak up for her and make a stand on her behalf that the tying of the sleeves was brought to light and stopped.

As a result everyone who worked with Susan was compelled to sit down and see Susan as a person and not as the 'problem and irritant' that constantly reminded them of their own shortcomings and failings. Things only started to improve for Susan when new strategies were adopted, which included enlisting the help of an outsider who very firmly advocated for Susan and continued to speak for her over a long period of time. Susan's advocate helped everyone to think of Susan as foremost the person she really was and not as 'the problem' that she presented. The resulting change in Susan was remarkable.

Mark

Mark was only four when he went to live in the same residential unit as Keith. Everyone expected him to die. He had many physical disabilities and cerebral palsy. Each winter he survived, each pound gained in weight, was a small triumph achieved with a struggle. He defied everyone's expectations. He had become separated from his family and saw them only infrequently. As he got stronger he began to grow and his wheelchair became too small. The specially moulded frame designed to support his twisted spine had now begun to pinch and squeeze his body. Usually he was not a complaining person but now he cried each time he was sat in the chair. As soon as he arrived at school, the staff would take him out and prop him up with cushions and wedges. This was a difficult position for Mark to sit in comfortably. School work became harder and harder to achieve. Mark on the whole did not make a fuss - he was interested in all that happened around him. The physio-therapist, the occupational therapist, the hostel staff, the school staff all agreed that he must have a new chair. Representations were made to all the correct departments, many times.

It was nearly a year before the new chair arrived. Bureaucracy and red tape caused endless delays and meanwhile a young child was being hurt each day.

Becoming an advocate

I doubt that these stories will be unfamiliar to staff who work in schools that cater for pupils with learning difficulties although they might be surprising to staff who work within the mainstream sector of education. The people who worked with Keith and Susan were not unkind people. They genuinely liked their work and wanted the best for their pupils. The bureaucrats making the regulations that denied Mark his wheel-chair for so long had no intention of hurting him. But the actions shown to Keith, Susan and Mark by those persons into whose care and trust they were placed must have raised some searching questions.

Why is it so hard for a member of the staff of a school to take on the role of an advocate and speak out on behalf of one of their pupils, even though they are only too aware of the injustices?

Keith and Susan's stories highlight the difficulties that all advocates have to face when confronted by what is a very real conflict of interest. Few school staff would be willing to jeopardise their own job security. Most would have strong feelings of loyalty to their colleagues and to the education system of which they are a part. Speaking out in this way can be interpreted as a challenge both to individual staff and to the school community of which, after all, the advocate is also a member. Taking such a stand may be seen as an act of subversion. It takes a strong person to resist the pressure from colleagues.

Those people who spoke out on behalf of Keith and Susan had a very uncomfortable time. They were called 'soft', 'busy-bodies', 'left-wingers', 'do-gooders'. In fact, only when the improvements began to show did the criticisms stop and attitudes gradually change. In the end everyone was trying to claim that they too had helped to bring about the remarkable change in Susan's behaviour.

Within the education system, the effectiveness of advocacy will al-ways be limited by the sheer power of the school system and its unwillingness to confront its own role in the exclusion, devaluation and oppression of young people like Keith, Susan, Mark and others. If school staff wish to seek realistic ways to redress these challenges, and to ensure that incidents such as I have described do not happen, then everyone must work both on the internal structures and practices within the school and call upon other external sources of advocacy if this should be thought necessary.

In a school it is unlikely that conflicts of interest can be entirely eliminated but they can be minimised. School staff, like anyone else wishing to act as an advocate, would benefit from being aware of likely sources of conflict. There may be many of these.

- To a member of the 'establishment', the survival of the service could be seen as being more important than the best interests of the service user, in this case, the pupil. Organisations may try to hush up or avoid scandal at the cost of doing nothing about the issue in question.
- Professionals may discourage promotion of the service user's interests, for example by defending the good name of the school at all costs.
- A member of staff has demands on his or her attention from every pupil. Giving more attention to one draws attention from the others.
- The interests of the 'service managers', in this situation the headteacher and senior staff, may differ from the grass-roots opinion of the school staff, or the parents' wishes. For instance, the pressure to 'keep the numbers up' may encourage tendencies towards accepting pupils at any price or obstructing the chance for pupils to move to different establishments that may suit individual needs better.
- Even if only advocating for one person, one's own personal needs, such as the need for a break, or the need for support from others, may be a source of conflict.

Different forms of advocacy

Self advocacy

For many, 'advocacy' is a buzz-word when it is linked to 'self advocacy'. In schools for pupils with learning difficulties, this may be given the status of a subject, with a regular slot in the timetable. It can conveniently be fitted into lessons under the heading of 'relationships', 'independence training' or 'personal growth and understanding'.

Self advocacy is often the only form of advocacy that most school staff are comfortable with or have heard of. In fact for the majority of people 'self advocacy is advocacy.' Generally people do not realise that self advocacy is only a part of the whole advocacy movement and that citizen advocacy, legal advocacy and collective or class advocacy are all very important processes that can be used to help people whose lives are at risk of being devalued.

Self advocacy is a term used when an individual acts on his or her own behalf to present their needs and concerns in a fairly formal way. It lends itself to being a perfect session on any school's timetable! Moreover, school staff still feel that they are in control of what is happening, or, as one teacher remarked to me after an afternoon self advocacy session spent encouraging a group of school leavers to talk openly about their plans and hopes for the future, 'It is only about giving them some practice in talking freely and making choices.' Unfortunately there was absolutely no guarantee that anyone would take any real notice of what had been said and act upon those students' wishes after that session had finished. In reality it had been designed as a communication session, with no real commitment or even understanding as to how to take things further.

Often for people with learning difficulties the opportunities to express their views, their likes and dislikes, are limited. It requires courage and confidence and there is no doubt that mutual support and comfort is given when individuals meet together in a group and learn the skills that will help them to speak out. The success of the People First movement, both here and in America, is testimony to this approach.

Self advocacy skills can be encouraged at an early age, when teachers intentionally include in their lesson plans opportunities for the pupils to make realistic choices during their regular lessons. It is all valuable experience helping to give the pupils more confidence and self awareness. School staff who adopt rigid attitudes towards their pupils, with fixed ideas over what is thought to be achievable by them, have problems when the pupils make their views known and start being assertive. Sometimes school staff have been observed to perceive this as a challenge to their integrity and to the effectiveness of their work, with the result that they take things far too personally.

For example, some staff have found it hard to accept that it is possible for students with learning difficulties to get paid work when they leave school, even before the present job climate made things so difficult for all school leavers. The result has been that the curriculum designed for the senior pupils may be heavily biased towards leisure activities and hobbies rather than emphasing skills that would help them to compete in the job market. In this way fundamental rights as citizens are overlooked or set aside.

In schools for pupils with learning difficulties, the technique of teaching in a one-to-one setting is widely used. This can encourage a dependency on adults that may stay with the pupils into adulthood and consequently make it difficult for them to make their real wishes known. Unless a balance is actively sought which uses other teaching methods that allow and encourage pupils to take responsibility for their own actions, they find themselves at a disadvantage when they grow up.

Teachers should not forget the powerful positions they hold.

There are other forms of advocacy which contribute to the process of advocacy. None is sufficient in itself to safeguard the interests of vulnerable people, but each is important and necessary.

Citizen advocacy

Citizen advocacy invites ordinary citizens to represent the interests of an individual who stands at risk of not being heard. It is a process that builds relationships between a vulnerable person and their family, or representatives of their service providers, so as to help tackle problems that they find too difficult or perhaps too painful to address in the usual way.

An advocate is impartial and is usually recruited and supported by a co-ordinator. Citizen advocates may find it easier to speak up for a pupil at an annual review in a way that family members and professionals find difficult to contemplate, being so deeply involved.

Legal advocacy

Legal advocates, because of their specialist knowledge, can confront the many breaches of fundamental rights of citizenship, to a degree that less well informed people cannot possibly contemplate.

Collective advocacy

Collective advocacy involves a group of people uniting to campaign on issues affecting more than one person. Examples include MENCAP, the Spastic Society, MIND or Greenpeace.

It should be obvious that none of these forms of advocacy can be thought of as subjects that can be put on the timetable. Only when school staff are aware of what advocacy means in all its forms; appreciate what is involved in being an advocate; understand the need for advocacy, and know how to set about encouraging effective advocacy for their pupils, will the many injustices endured every day by their pupils stand a chance of being brought to light.

Raising issues

It is easy to focus on the major injustices. The stories of Keith, Susan and Mark show us that vigilance is needed all the time to tackle the issues, big and small, that lead to infringments of pupils' interests often not immediately obvious and ignored. There are many common examples.

- In most schools for pupils with learning difficulties dissatisfaction over the arrangements for the transportation of pupils to and from school is regularly expressed. Pupils are missing vital school time when the taxis arrive either late in the morning or too early in the afternoon and this will mount up during the terms and throughout the years into days or weeks of lost school time. Denying proper education to a child for days or weeks at a time is to deny fundamental rights (and to flout the law).
- Consider the quantity and quality of the school meal service. Menus for school lunches seem to be budgeted for as if all the pupils were of primary school age but in reality a good 50 per cent of the population of many schools for pupils with learning difficulties are teenagers and have appetites to match.
- People dependent on a wheelchair often experience constant hanging around and time spent waiting. It is a common sight to see pupils sitting and waiting - to be pushed to the dining room for lunch, probably to start their dinner early; to go to their next class; or just waiting for the 'pusher' before they can catch up with the rest of their classmates. How much time is wasted in their lives?
- Imagine being taken to the toilet when you don't really want to go, but it is the time that is convenient for the staff and fits into their routines.
- There is an appalling lack of choice as to what is available when students leave school - the day centres or nothing. The education service seems to believe that once pupils have left school it is no longer their responsibility to worry. There is an amazing ability to 'pass the buck' between the services, coupled with a reluctance to co-operate amongst the professionals.

Lastly it is all too easy for advocacy, in all its forms, to be confused with the range of good, but nevertheless partial techniques, that also try to safeguard the interests of individuals. Schemes such as caseworkers, keyworkers, quality assurance, and volunteers are all useful and have a place in the battle to improve the lives of devalued people. But the partiality of these schemes make them very different from advocacy.

To be effective, advocacy must be as independent as possible and it is precisely this emphasis on independence that makes it such a powerful relationship. The less conflict of interest the more effective the advocacy.

True advocacy, allowing independent advocates to speak on behalf of pupils, is a challenging concept that some schools are beginning to accept. It is understandable that self advocacy should be an easy and natural starting point but it is time to move on. We know that some pupils may never be able to speak up clearly for themselves and for the forseeable future are always going to be reliant on someone else's support and vigilance to safeguard their interests and minimise the injustices they so often have to endure.

Being seen as a friend standing alongside a person that has been rejected by others conveys a very powerful message which challenges intolerance and injustice to the core. It should not be underestimated.

Everyone involved in special education needs to ask themselves, and repeat these questions every working day:

- What fundamental injustices here have we grown so used to seeing that they no longer catch our attention? How can we become sensitive to what really goes on in our schools and in the pupils' lives?
- When we see injustice, what stops us acting? How can we work together in ways that support special educators becoming effective advocates and enable advocacy in all its forms to be welcomed in our schools?

Notes: For further reading, look at the contributions made by Jupp, K. and Tyne, A. (1993) to *The Great Integration Debate,* BIMH Publications, Vol. 21, (2), (3) and at *Citizen Advocacy, a Powerful Partnership* published by National Citizen Advocacy (1988) of Unit 2K, Leroy House, 436, Essex Road, London. N1 3QP. Tel: 071 359 8289.

People First can be contacted at 207 - 215, King's Cross Road, London. WC1X 9DB. Tel: 071 713 6400.

References

Ackerman, D. and Mount, H. (1991) *Literacy for All.* London: Fulton.

Aherne, P., Thornber, A., Fagg, S. and Skelton, S. (1990a) *Communication for All.* London: Fulton.

Aherne, P., Thornber, A., Fagg, S. and Skelton, S. (1990b) *Mathematics for All: an Interactive Approach within Level 1.* London: Fulton.

Ainscow, M. (1988) 'No Time for Knee Jerks.' *Special Children.* Issue 22, June, p. 24-25.

Alexander, R., Rose, J. and Woodhead, C. (1992) *Curriculum Organisation and Classroom Practice in Primary Schools.* DES: HMSO.

Banes, D. and Sebba, J. (1991) 'I Was Little Then: Accessing History for Pupils with Severe Learning Difficulties.' *British Journal of Special Education,* 18, (3), 121-124.

Bender, M. P. (1976) *Community Psychology.* London: Methuen.

Bignell, L. (1991) 'The Way Ahead.' In Ashdown, R., Carpenter, B. and Bovair, K. (eds) *The Curriculum Challenge.* London: Falmer.

Byers, R. (1992) 'Topics: from myths to objectives.' In Bovair, K., Carpenter, B. and Upton, G. (eds) *Special Curricula Needs.* London: Fulton.

Carpenter, B. (1991a) *Symbol Stories - an information sheet for teachers, assistants and parents.* Education Dept. PO Box 20, Council House, Solihull.

Carpenter, B. (1991b) 'Unlocking the door: access to English in the National Curriculum.' In Smith, B. (ed) *Interactive Approaches to the Core Subjects.* Bristol: Lame Duck Press.

Carpenter, B. (1992) 'The whole curriculum: meeting the needs of the whole child.' In Bovair, K., Carpenter, B. and Upton, G. (eds) *Special Curricula Needs.* London: Fulton.

Coupe, J. and Goldbart, J. (1988) *Communication before Speech*. London: Croom Helm.

Coupe, J. and Joliffe, J. (1988) 'An early communication curriculum: implications for practice.' In Coupe, J. and Goldbart, J. *Communication before Speech*. London: Croom Helm.

Craft, A. (1991) *Living Your Life; a Sex Education and Personal Development Programme for Students with Severe Learning Difficulties*. Wisbech: LDA.

Dearing, Sir R. (1993a) 'Foreword.' In National Curriculum Council *Planning the National Curriculum at Key Stage 2*. York: NCC.

Dearing Sir R. (1993b) *The National Curriculum and its Assessment - an Interim Report*. York/London: NCC/SEAC.

Dee, L. (1988) *New Directions*. London: F.E.U.

DES (1988) *The Education Reform Act*. London: HMSO.

DES (1989a) *Planning for School Development*. London: HMSO

DES and Welsh Office (1989b) *English in the National Curriculum*. London: HMSO

DES (1991) *Assessment, Recording and Reporting in Special Schools*. A Report by H.M. Inspectors. London: HMSO.

Fagg, S., Aherne, P., Skelton, S., and Thornber, A. (1990) *Entitlement for All in Practice*. London: Fulton.

Fagg, S., Skelton, S., Aherne, P., and Thornber, A. (1990) *Science for All*. London: Fulton.

Friere, P. (1972) *Pedagogy of the Oppressed*. Harmondsworth: Penguin.

George Hastwell School (1992) *George Hastwell News* (school newspaper, October 1992), Barrow-in-Furness, Cumbria.

Goldbart, J. (1990) 'Preintentional communication: opening the communication curriculum to students with profound and multiple learning difficulties.' Paper presented to the International Special Education Congress: Cardiff.

Gummett, B. and Martin, C. (1992) *Global Concepts*, (newsletter of Northwest SEMERC), copy 5, summer, pp 3-4 .

Howe, L. (1991) 'Approaches to science.' In Ashdown, R., Carpenter, B. and Bovair, K. (eds) *The Curriculum Challenge: Access to the National Curriculum for Pupils with Learning Difficulties*. London: Falmer.

Kolb, D. (1984) *Experiential Learning - Experience as the Source of Learning and Development*. New Jersey: Prentice-Hall.

Kopchick, G. A. and Lloyd, L. L. (1976) 'Total communication programming for the severely language impaired: a 24-hour approach.' In Lloyd, L. L. (ed) *Communication Assessment and Intervention Strategies*. Maryland: University Park Press.

Lacey, P., Smith, B. and Tilstone, C. (1991) 'Influences on curriculum design and on assessment.' In Tilstone C. (ed) *Teaching Pupils with Severe Learning Difficulties*. London: Fulton.

Lawson, H. (1992) *Practical Record Keeping for Special Schools*. London: Fulton.

MacConville, R. and Bowers, M. (1993) Review of 'Redefining the Whole Curriculum for Pupils with Learning Difficulties' *Eye Contact,* Summer, 22-23.

McConkey, R. (1987) 'Interaction: the name of the game.' In Smith, B. (ed) *Interactive Approaches to the Education of Children with Severe Learning Difficulties.* Birmingham: Westhill College.

McLean, J. and Snyder-McLean, L. (1985) 'Developmentally early communicative behaviours among severely mentally retarded adolescents.' Seminar topic, Hester Adrian Research Centre, University of Manchester.

Mittler, P. (1988) 'Foreword.' In Coupe, J. and Goldbart, J. *Communication before Speech.* London: Croom Helm.

Mittler, P. (1990) 'From Entitlement to Access.' In Fagg, S., Aherne, P., Skelton, S. and Thornber, A. *Entitlement for All in Practice.* London: Fulton.

Mount, H. and Ackerman, D. (1991) *Technology for All.* London: Fulton.

Mulligan, J. (1992) 'Internal Processors in Experiential Learning'. In Mulligan, J. and Griffin, C. (eds) *Empowerment throught Experiential Learning - Explorations of Good Practice.* London: Kogan Page.

National Curriculum Council (1990a) *Curriculum Guidance 3: The Whole Curriculum.* York: NCC.

National Curriculum Council (1990b) *Curriculum Guidance 6: Careers Education and Guidance.* York: NCC.

National Curriculum Council (1992a) *Curriculum Guidance 9: The National Curriculum and Pupils with Severe Learning Difficulties.* York: NCC.

National Curriculum Council (1992b) *The National Curriculum and Pupils with Severe Learning Difficulties: INSET Resources.* York: NCC

National Curriculum Council (1992c) *Curriculum Guidance 10: Teaching Science to Pupils with Special Educational Needs.* York: NCC.

National Curriculum Council (1993a) *The National Curriculum at Key Stages 1 and 2.* York: NCC.

National Curriculum Council (1993b) *Planning the National Curriculum at Key Stage 2.* York: NCC.

Newman, K. and Rose, R. (1991) 'Self Evaluation at Wren Spinney.' *British Journal of Special Education,* 17, (1), 12-14.

Nielsen, L. (1992) *Educational Approaches for Visually Impaired Children.* Copenhagen: SIKON.

Nind, M. and Hewett, D. (1988) 'Interaction as curriculum.' *British Journal of Special Education,* 15, (2), 55-57.

Norwich, B. 1989. 'How should we define exceptions ?' *British Journal of Special Education.* 16, (3), 94-97.

Ockelford, A. (1993) *Objects of Reference.* London: RNIB.

OECD/CERI (1986) *Young People with Handicaps: The Road to Adulthood.* Paris: OECD.

OFSTED (1993a) *Curriculum Practice and Classroom Practice in Primary Schools.* London: HMSO.

OFSTED (1993b) *Handbook for the Inspection of Schools.* London: HMSO.

OFSTED (1993c) *Special Needs and the National Curriculum.* London: HMSO.

Ouvry, C. (1991) 'Access for pupils with profound and multiple learning difficulties.' In Ashdown, R., Carpenter, B. and Bovair, K. (eds) *The Curriculum Challenge: Access to the National Curriculum for Pupils with Learning Difficulties.* London: Falmer.

Pease, L., and Chapman, N. (1992) 'Disapply First, Modify Later?' *British Journal of Special Education,* 19, (3), 103-104.

Peter, M. (1993) 'Editorial', *British Journal of Special Education.* 20, (1), 3.

Pring, P. (1990) *The New Curriculum.* London: Cassell.

Rogers, C. (1983) *Freedom to Learn for the 80's.* Columbus, Ohio: Charles E. Merrill Publishing Co.

Rose, R. (1991) 'A jigsaw approach to group work.' *British Journal of Special Education,* 18, (2), 54-58.

Rose, R. (1992) 'Entitlement and access to science in the curriculum for pupils with special needs.' In Atlay, M., Bennett, S., Dutch, S., Levinson, R., Taylor, R. and West, R. (eds) *Open Chemistry.* London: Hodder and Stoughton.

Ryder, J. and Campbell, L. (1988) *Balancing Acts in Personal, Social and Health Education.* London: Routledge.

Sebba, J. and Fergusson, A. (1991) 'Reducing the marginalisation of pupils with severe learning difficulties through curricular initiatives.' In Ainscow, M. (ed) *Effective Schools for All.* London: Fulton.

Sebba, J., Galloway, S. and Rodbard, G. (1991) *Water - An Integrated Approach to Meeting the Needs of Pupils with Profound and Multiple Learning Difficulties within the National Curriculum: A Resource Pack for Teachers.* Hertford: Hertfordshire County Council.

Sebba, J. and Clarke, J. (1991) 'Meeting the needs of pupils within history and geography', In Ashdown, R., Carpenter, B. and Bovair, K. (eds). *The Curriculum Challenge: Access to the National Curriculum for Pupils with Learning Difficulties.* London: Falmer.

Sebba, J. and Clarke, J. (1993) 'Practical approaches to increasing access to geography.' *Support for Learning,* 8, (2), 70-76.

Sebba, J., Byers, R. and Rose, R. (1993) *Redefining the Whole Curriculum for Pupils with Learning Difficulties.* London: Fulton.

Staff of Blythe School (1986) *Working with Makaton at Blythe School.* Camberley: Makaton Vocabulary Development Project.

Staff of Tye Green School (1991) 'Broad, Balanced and Relevant?' *Special Children.* 44, 11-13.

Thomas, G. (1993) Review of 'Redefining the Whole Curriculum for Pupils with Learning Difficulties' *Times Educational Supplement,* June 11th 1993, p. 14.

Tilstone, C. (1991) 'Pupils' Views.' In Tilstone, C. (ed) *Teaching Pupils with Severe Learning Difficulties.* London: Fulton.

van Oosterom, J. (1991) 'Aspects of English.' In Ashdown, R., Carpenter, B. and Bovair, K. (eds) *The Curriculum Challenge: Access to the National Curriculum for Pupils with Learning Difficulties.* London: Falmer.

Vernon, V. A. (1993) Letter in *PMLD Link,* (16), Summer edition.

Ware, J. (1990) 'The National Curriculum for pupils with severe learning difficulties.' In Daniels, H. and Ware, J. (eds) *Special Educational Needs and the National Curriculum.* London: Kogan Page.

Wedell, K. (1988) 'The New Act: a special need for vigilance.' *British Journal of Special Education,* 15, (3), 98-101.

Author Index

Subject Index

164

Recording   18, 25, 51, 58–60,
    68, 95, 119, 121–128,
    129–144.
Records of Achievement   17, 25,
    50, 60, 62, 68, 129–144.
Religious education   18.
Reporting   18, 130.
Resources   33, 42, 52, 53, 56, 61,
    77, 80–85.
Rewards   94, 118–119, 141.
Rights and responsibilities   20,145,
    151–152, 153.

School development planning
    46–47.
School rules   30.
SCAA (Schools Curriculum and
    Assessment Authority)   7, 9.
SEAC (Schools Examination and
    Assessment Council)   7.
Science   17, 18, 50, 54, 56, 103.
Self esteem   30, 33, 59, 100, 107.
Sensory exploration   18, 21.
Sex education   30–31.
Signs/signing   76–86, 148.
Spastics Society, The   vii, 63, 152.
Staff development   16–17, 51, 64,
    68–72, 77.
Subject focused teaching   54, 121,
    122, 125, 127, 145.

Support staff   xiv, 65, 68, 70–71,
    72.
Symbols   21, 56, 58, 66, 75, 76–86,
    98, 110, 131, 133–138, 144.

Teaching approaches and learning
    styles   x, 8, 17–18, 32, 42–43,
    44, 50, 58, 74, 99–102,
    107–120, 151–152.
Team teaching   51, 64–65, 67–68,
    108.
Technology   17, 18, 24, 50, 92, 115,
    130.
Therapy   xiv, 46, 67, 71.
  physiotherapy   25, 36, 63, 65, 67,
    68, 148.
  occupational therapy   36, 65, 67,
    148.
  speech therapy   15, 36, 65, 67, 68.
Time management   49, 53, 54–56,
    94, 123, 127–128.
TVEI (Technical and Vocational
    Education Initiative)   17, 50.
Twenty-four hour curriculum   77.

Whole curriculum   x, 30–31, 35,
    37, 63–72, 73, 74, 93, 116, 122.
Whole pupil/student/person   108,
    109, 111–114, 116, 130.
Work experience   17, 18, 30.